Wallace Stegner

Wallace Stegner

DEAN OF WESTERN WRITERS

ALEX BEAM

SIGNATURE BOOKS | 2025 | SALT LAKE CITY

To my friend David Roberts, (1943–2021)
a lover, explorer, and chronicler of Wallace Stegner's West

Join our mailing list at signaturebooks.com for details on events and related titles we think you'll enjoy

Cover image: *Wallace Stegner* by Trent Call, from *Iconoclasts* by Ken Sanders.

Frontispiece photo used by permission, Utah Historical Society.

Design by Jason Francis

FIRST EDITION | 2025

Paperback ISBN: 978-1-56085-519-4
Ebook ISBN: 978-1-56085-500-2

Contents

"Someone asked me recently, 'Who is your favorite living American writer?' I said, 'Wallace Stegner.'"
—David McCullough, 1990

Introduction

"A stray, he yearned to belong." —*Recapitulation*

Wallace Stegner's first coherent memory was of the Sacred Heart orphanage on Seattle's Beacon Hill. He recalled "the musty, buttery odor" of the stale bread crusts served as midmorning snacks. Stegner was a small, skinny child, prone to crying. "I never got any [bread] because I was little," he recalled, "and once in a while my brother would take pity on me and give me a bite."

His parents had temporarily separated after the café they were managing failed. His father, George, had lit off with a gambling acquaintance for British Columbia. Stegner's mother, Hilda, worked at the Bon Marche department store but found herself unable to both work and care for her two sons. She deposited them at Sacred Heart, which Stegner remembered as a "dump. It was literally an asylum of the old-fashioned kind."[1]

If there is one recurring theme in Stegner's work, it is his search for a home. "If you don't know where you are, you don't know who you are," was his student Wendell Berry's famous remark about the interconnection between place and self-knowledge.

Stegner's life was a successive discovery of homes—from his boyhood in Saskatchewan's Cypress Hills, to Salt Lake City, where he matured from an adolescent to a young man, to Stanford University and Los Altos Hills, where he taught and lived for almost fifty years. He chose Greensboro, Vermont, where he owned a summer home for over sixty years, as his final resting place. It was also the setting for his last novel.

Wallace Stegner started writing as a young man and lived to be

1. Philip Fradkin, *Wallace Stegner and the American West* (New York: Alfred A. Knopf, 2008), 13–14.

eighty-seven years old. He published his first story in *The Salt Lake Tribune* in 1934; he published his last novel, *Crossing to Safety*, in 1987, six years before his death. All told, Stegner wrote fourteen novels, two excellent biographies, two memorable works of Mormon history, and dozens of short stories and essays collected into books.

He was born with a nineteenth-century sensibility often at odds with the cultural trends that irked him at the end of his life. His biographer Jackson Benson notes that "Stegner was probably the only important writer living into the 1990s who actually experienced the pioneering period of North American history, on the last unsettled frontier."[2]

Vita longa, ars longa.

Stegner often compared himself to the diligent beaver: "A talent is a kind of imprisonment," he once explained. "You're stuck in it, you have to keep using it, or else you get ruined by it. It's like a beaver's teeth. He has to chew or else his jaws lock shut."[3]

Stegner would have been the first to admit that his work was uneven. He disavowed two of his youthful novels, refusing to see them reprinted. "*On a Darkling Plain* embarrasses me," he told an interviewer. "*Fire and Ice* rather embarrasses me, too."[4] As a young man, he needed money and wrote a lot—a habit he never shook. In 1945, he published a rosy-toned "portrait of America" called *One Nation*, intended as a wartime morale booster. In 1971 he published a book about ARAMCO, the Arabian-American Oil Company, financed by the corporation itself. Many of his essays about his upbringing, and about the fate of the West, repeat themselves—in part because as a mature writer he was deluged with requests for commentaries and contributions. Who could resist repolishing some previous works now and again?

The scut work is okay, the good work is good, and Stegner's great work is great. He won a Pulitzer Prize for his 1971 novel *Angle of*

---

2. Jackson Benson, *Wallace Stegner: His Life and Work* (New York: Viking Penguin, 1996), 21.

3. Patricia Rowe Willrich, "A Perspective on Wallace Stegner," *Virginia Quarterly Review* 67, no. 2 (Spring 1991): 240–59.

4. Richard W. Etulain and Wallace Stegner, *Conversations with Wallace Stegner on Western History and Literature*, revised edition (Salt Lake City: University of Utah Press, 1990), 36.

Repose, and a National Book Award for *The Spectator Bird*, published five years later. It was whispered that he would have won an earlier Pulitzer for his magisterial biography of Western explorer and cartographer John Wesley Powell, if only his friend Bernard DeVoto hadn't used the introduction to vilify a recent Pulitzer-winning historian of the West.[5] Die-hard Stegnerians might argue that he wrote even better books than these, such as his 1974 DeVoto biography, *The Uneasy Chair*, or his vivid and admiring account of the 1846 Mormon trek, *The Gathering of Zion* (1964).

My personal favorite among his books is the wistful and erudite *Crossing to Safety*, which a *New York Times* reviewer called "a superb book at the ... end of a consistently accomplished career."[6]

No one would call Stegner an experimental writer—he inveighed against experimental prose in his later years—yet he crossed genre boundaries more often than many critics realize. *Wolf Willow*, the memoir of his Saskatchewan boyhood, is part Andy-of-Mayberry-style recollections of small-town life admixed with some serious history of the Canadian Mounties, and of the Northern Plains Indians who crossed the "Medicine Line" from the United States into Canada. *Willow* also includes an eighty-page novella, *Genesis*, which Stegner's student Larry McMurtry called "as good a short novel as anybody has done about the West, or any part of it." Stegner sardonically called *Willow* "a librarian's nightmare. How do you catalogue it?"[7]

Stegner believed history could be—should be—"novelistic," not meaning fictional, but at least as interesting to read as a good novel. His first popular history, *Mormon Country*, published in 1942, included fictional vignettes. "My intention in *The Gathering of Zion* was clearly novelistic in its emphasis on human interest," Stegner explained, "but historical in that I wanted to be faithful to fact and record. *Because I was after visceral history*."[8] Instead of writing a conventional biography of the famed labor organizer Joe Hill, he wrote a "biographical novel" in 1969.

5. Benson, *Wallace Stegner*, 224.

6. Doris Grumbach, "The Grace of Old Lovers," *The New York Times*, Sep. 20, 1987.

7. Wallace Stegner, *Wolf Willow: A History, a Story, and a Memory of the Last Plains Frontier* (New York: Penguin Classics, 2000), xi.

8. Wallace Stegner, "On the Writing of History," in *The Sound of Mountain Water* (New York: Vintage, 2017), 208. Emphasis mine.

Stegner's casual border-crossings between fact and fiction would land him in a heap of trouble when he integrated huge swathes of Mary Hallock Foote's diaries, verbatim, into his Pulitzer-winning *Angle of Repose*.

Writing was not Stegner's only career. He worked at universities most of his life, most notably at Stanford as the founding director of the Stegner Fellowship creative writing program. There he mentored fledgling writers who would later bejewel the literary firmament like the seed of Abraham: Tillie Olsen, Ernest Gaines, Thomas McGuane, Evan Connell, Wendell Berry, Ken Kesey, Larry McMurtry, and Edward Abbey are just a few of them.

He was also a tireless advocate for the proper use of Western lands, a pursuit that used to be called, primly, "conservation." Stegner worked as a special assistant to Secretary of the Interior Stewart Udall in 1961, and also served on the board of the Sierra Club and on the National Parks Advisory Board. Often in league with DeVoto, Stegner made himself heard on the land use issues of the day, mostly involving proposed dams deemed integral to the development of the arid Intermountain West.

Stegner had an abundance of other talents. For instance, he was an accomplished carpenter, who assembled much of the original framing for his Los Altos Hills house by himself, as help was hard to come by in post-World War II 1946. With a friend, he shingled his summer home in Greensboro. He must have been quite useful to have around the house. A high school basketballer and a varsity tennis player in college, he later developed an affinity for badminton, a serious sport not taken very seriously in the United States.

So here is Wallace Stegner, the man in full, in brief. It is worth noting that Stegner fictionalized much of his own biography. His first major novel, *The Big Rock Candy Mountain*, is a barely veiled account of his adolescence and young adulthood in Salt Lake City. He returned to Salt Lake City in his 1979 novel, *Recapitulation*, a re-remembering of his formative years among the Mormons. The generally solid "Joe Allston" novels, *All the Little Live Things* (1967) and *The Spectator Bird* (1976), set in the Northern California Peninsula foothills near Palo Alto, also echo many themes of Stegner's biography. Readers can learn about Stegner's life from these "auto-fictions" and from two excellent Stegner biographies: Jackson Benson's *Wallace Stegner: His Life and Work* (1986) and Philip Fradkin's *Wallace Stegner and the American West* (2008).

Stegner was often interviewed, and his lengthy exchanges with University of Mexico professor (now emeritus) Richard Etulain, and with James Hepworth, both collected into books,[9] are invaluable troves of Stegner-iana.

Biographies don't have to "tell all." Stegner himself hand-waved the final years of his hero John Wesley Powell, explaining that once Powell started writing dense, unapproachable tomes, the biographer lost interest: "With his philosophy of science, his epistemology, this book has nothing to do."[10] I have made similar choices here. For instance, I hate biographies that are padded with plot summaries of an author's books. I have tried to avoid those. I'm not a Stegner completist. If I describe a book, I've read it, but when the author himself warns you away from some of his early fiction, I take heed. I'll briefly describe the consequential works, but almost without exception, you should pick them up on your own.

What a hard worker Stegner was! What an enviable career he had; and what a principled life he led. Even his sternest critics would allow that he wrote half a dozen books very much worth reading. How many authors can claim that? Stegner is a writer who is far greater than the sum of his impressive parts.

9. Etulain and Stegner, *Conversations with Wallace Stegner*; James R. Hepworth, *Stealing Glances: Three Interviews with Wallace Stegner* (Albuquerque, NM: University of New Mexico Press, 1980).

10. Wallace Stegner, *Beyond the 100th Meridian: John Wesley Powell and the Second Opening of the West* (New York: Penguin, 1992), 348.

ONE

Beginnings

"There are certain advantages to growing up a sensuous little savage." —*Wolf Willow*

Wallace Stegner's sentient life began in Eastend, Saskatchewan, where his family moved in 1914. He was five years old. By his son Page's account, Wallace's family had already moved five times: "He, his mother, and his brother Cecil arrived in the summer of 1914 to rejoin his father, living in a derailed dining car for over a year until George finally built a small, gabled white frame house."[1]

The railway car was "considered pretty classy," Wallace remembered. "Later we lived in a rented shack." The young Wallace shot gophers manically and, several years in a row, won prizes for presenting the most tails in a schoolboy competition. He received an elementary education in a school located above the local pool hall, and then in a tiny, brick schoolhouse. "Mark Twain, confronted by a colorful character, used to say, 'I know him—knew him on the river.' I could say, about as legitimately, 'I know him—knew him in Eastend.' A young frontier gathers every sort of migrant, hope-chaser roughneck, trickster, incompetent misfit and failure."[2]

His father, George, had a homestead claim fifty miles outside of town where he hoped to make a killing raising wheat, the price of which had spiked during World War I. Stegner's long-suffering mother, Hilda, was trapped in an unhappy marriage to a volatile,

1. Wallace Stegner, *Wolf Willow: A History, a Story, and a Memory of the Last Plains Frontier* (New York: Penguin Classics, 2000), xvii.

2. Wallace Stegner, *Growing Up Western*, typescript, box 141, fd. 2, Wallace Stegner Papers, J. Willard Marriott Library, University of Utah, Salt Lake City.

occasionally violent husband. When George abandoned her for the first time in Seattle, she asked her father if she could divorce him. A devout Lutheran, he answered that adultery was the only grounds for dissolving a marriage. She persevered.[3]

Wallace spent the summer months helping his father work the farm, and the rest of the year in the town's school. Life in the farm's one-room shack was rudimentary. There was no electricity, no ice box, "and no shade," Stegner recalled. The family stored milk under the floorboards, where it kept cool for perhaps half a day.[4]

Money was scarce. On one particularly lean Christmas, Stegner recalled, "my brother and I fell silent and ashamed when on Christmas morning other kids came around to show off their presents." He and Cecil had each received a pencil box, home-knit stockings, and homemade shirts his mother had fashioned from the lining of a discarded coat.[5]

Stegner, who would grow up to be an imposing adult ("His friends said he looked like God ought to look," one critic wrote[6]), was a weakling child. "I was a crybaby. My circulation was poor and my hands always got blue and white in the cold. I always had a runny nose."[7] Stegner made it clear that the cultural backwater of Eastend was highly unlikely to produce a future prize-winning writer, calling it "a dunghole sagebrush town on the disappearing edge of nowhere, utterly without painting, without sculpture, without architecture ... almost without books."[8]

George Stegner would not make his fortune in wheat. Three scorching summers saw to that. A gambler and a main chancer whose homestead plot abutted Canada's southern border, he had some experience ferrying liquor south into the United States. Appraising "dry" Salt Lake City as an appealing venue for the hooch trade, George uprooted his family again and planted his flag in the shadow of the

3. Philip Fradkin, *Wallace Stegner and the American West* (Berkeley, CA: University of California Press, 2009), 15.

4. Jackson Benson, *Wallace Stegner: His Life and Work* (New York: Viking Penguin, 1996), 20.

5. Stegner, *Wolf Willow*, 261.

6. Timothy Egan, "Stegner's Complaint," *The New York Times*, Feb. 18, 2009.

7. Stegner, *Wolf Willow*, 130.

8. Stegner, *Wolf Willow*, 24.

Wasatch range. Here is a fictionalized version of the Stegner family's "This is the place" moment from *The Big Rock Candy Mountain*:

> Early the next afternoon they rolled around the base of Ensign Peak and looked upon the city of the Saints.
>
> "Gee," Bruce said, standing up to see better, "This is a big town."
>
> "Isn't it nice?" Elsa said. "It's like all the towns through here, so green and nice."

Bo Mason, the fictionalized George Stegner, notes that there is a "whiskey famine" in Salt Lake City; "an active city prohibition force called the Purity Squad ... had steered the whiskey supply to other points." "Holy cats," Bo Mason exclaims. "I could sell whiskey in this town as fast as I could haul it in."[9]

Improbably, George Stegner was about to embark on a two-decade-long career as a bootlegger and proprietor of a "blind pig"—a speakeasy—in Mormon Salt Lake City.

Wallace Stegner believed in environmental and genealogical determinism, at least where his own biography is concerned. "Any person is an exercise in genealogy," he wrote in *Big Rock Candy Mountain*.[10] By genealogy, Stegner meant his parents. And the parent who weighed on him like an anchor around his neck was his father.

George Stegner "was a boomer from the age of fourteen, always on the lookout for the big chance, the ground floor, the inside track," Wallace wrote.[11] "George tried professional baseball, ran a lunchroom in Seattle, and even spent a few years as a wheat farmer.... Rainbows flowered for my father in every sky he looked at; he was led by pillars of fire and cloud."

Stegner cast his father as his personal tormentor. In fiction and in real life, George favored Wallace's athletic older brother, Cecil, over his more studious younger son. Wallace himself became a reasonable

9. Wallace Stegner, *The Big Rock Candy Mountain,* revised edition (New York: Penguin Classics, 2010), 369 ff. In his biography, Benson explains (130–31) that *The Big Rock Candy Mountain* is essentially non-fiction: "The work is so closely based on Stegner's life that it is difficult even for the biographer to find those few differences that mark the book as fiction, and it is difficult not to talk about the events in the book as if they happened to the author, since almost all of them did."

10. Stegner, *Big Rock*, 436.

11. Wallace Stegner, *Where the Bluebird Sings to the Lemonade Springs: Living and Writing in the West*, reprint edition (New York: Random House Publishing Group, 2002), xxv.

sportsman, playing varsity tennis in high school and college, but that never counted for much with his father. Stegner worked the complaint even further, turning his father into a dybbuk, an evil spirit that not only haunted Wallace's life, but became an emblem of everything that was wrong with life in the West—the entire universe for Wallace Stegner. Both as a novelist and an essayist, Stegner inveighed tirelessly (and sometimes tiresomely) against the get-rich-quick boomer mentality embodied by George Stegner.

Biographer Jackson Benson explained that a dichotomy developed in Stegner's mind between "the proud, tough, intolerant rugged individualism represented by his father and the friendly, tolerant, neighborly tendencies toward caring and cooperation represented by his mother." According to Benson, Stegner saw the conflict between his parents "as a synecdoche for the Western clash between the forces of rugged individualism on the one side and the forces of cooperation and community on the other."[12]

"Stegner would spend much of his life trying to exorcise the pain his father had caused him by using literature as therapy—'writing him out of my system,' as he once put it," Wallace's friend Thomas Watkins wrote. "By the end of his life, he thought he had managed to do it. I'm not so sure he had."[13]

George hounded his son for money throughout his life, even in the months before his death in 1939. On February 1, George wrote: "Well Wallace if you have some money to spare ..." On February 17: "Did you get my letter? ... things are tougher than *hell* here."[14] February 27: "I rec'd your letter and check ..."[15]

The end of George Stegner's life was demonic, and the details spread across all three of Salt Lake's daily newspapers. On June 15, 1939, George, who may or may not have been pursuing a mining venture in Nevada, obtained a police permit to carry a pearl-handled revolver. Later that day, he used the gun during an altercation at the Heron Hotel with Dorothy LeRoy, an attractive, thirty-eight-year-old divorcee, who may or may not have been both a financial

12. Benson, *Wallace Stegner*, 22.

13. Wallace Stegner, *Crossing to Safety*, reprint edition (New York: Modern Library, 2002), 330.

14. Emphasis in original.

15. Box 2, fd. 1, Wallace Stegner Papers.

backer and a paramour. She hit him with her pocketbook; he shot her through the heart and then turned the gun on himself. *The Salt Lake Tribune* reported that George Stegner's only surviving son, Wallace, was teaching at the University of Wisconsin.

Wallace's mother, brother, and father are all buried in the northwest section of Salt Lake City Cemetery. Only George's grave is unmarked, as his surviving son adamantly refused to pay for a headstone.[16]

If Wallace demonized his father, he worshipped the memory of his mother, Hilda. Diagnosed with breast cancer in her forties, Hilda had a double mastectomy in Salt Lake City and withdrew even further from the tumultuous goings-on at her husband's speakeasy. "I was at heart a nester, like my mother," Stegner wrote.[17] He was. When the 37-year-old Wallace arrived in Palo Alto to work at Stanford University in 1946, he stayed planted for the next forty-seven years. In an essay addressed to his mother, "Letter, Much Too Late," he bemoans Hilda's "fatal love choice."[18] Like many sons, he concluded that he had lived in rebellion against his father, while desperately trying to honor his mother's memory: "I would never get over trying, however badly or sadly or confusedly, to be what you thought I was," he wrote.[19]

That was the genealogy. Now for the environment.

Salt Lake City, to paraphrase another great American novelist, became Stegner's Yale College and his Harvard. Stegner believed that where his parents failed to raise him—his father indifferent, his tormented mother incapable—the Mormons stepped in.

All his life he sang the praises of the Mormon Mutual Improvement Association, which organized salubrious activities for young people, such as teenage dances, Boy Scout meetings, and basketball games on weekday evenings. "For three or four winters, with a club basketball team, I ran myself ragged in the frigid amusement halls of a hundred Mormon ward houses," he recalled. "There may have been a covert proselytizing motive in the welcome that the wards

16. Fradkin, 94–95.
17. Stegner, *Bluebird*, 12.
18. Stegner, *Bluebird*, 25.
19. Stegner, *Bluebird*, 23.

extended to strange gentile kids, but there was a lot of plain warmth and goodwill, too. . . . What I wanted most, it seems to me now, was to belong, and Mormon institutions are made to order for belongers."[20]

Belonging became the great theme of Stegner's life. In *Crossing to Safety*, the Stegner stand-in protagonist, Larry Morgan, airs his desperate urge to be accepted in his new home of Madison, Wisconsin: "What the disorderly crave above everything is order, *what the dislocated aspire to is location.* Reading my way out of disaster in the Berkeley library, I had run into Henry Adams. 'Chaos,' he told me, 'is the law of nature; order is the dream of man.'"[21]

"I spent my youth envying people who had lived all their lives in the houses they were born in, and had attics full of proof that they *had* lived."[22]

The Mormons, with their quadratically platted frontier cities and their mille-feuille-tiered layers of celestial existence, are an orderly lot, and their social ideology—if not their theology—resonated with young Wally. Case in point: The Mormons loved scouting. Stegner loved scouting, which allowed him to exercise his natural industry and ambition. "Once in the Boy Scouts," he wrote, "I went up through the ranks to eagle like smoke up a chimney."[23] Or his high school ROTC program. Stegner desperately wanted to participate, but he didn't weigh the minimum one hundred pounds. So he ate ferociously to gain weight, and soon "I had my moment of glory when, in Sam Browne belt, leather puttees, shoulder pips and sword, I led a platoon down Main Street in the Decoration Day parade."

Maybe the University of Utah in the mid-1920s wasn't yet Yale College, but it was a terrific place for a hungry mind. Benson called "the U" a "streetcar school," "a happy and relaxed place that exuded a spirit of optimism—Western optimism, Mormon optimism, youthful optimism."[24] The novelist Vardis Fisher talent-spotted Stegner in freshman English. "Fisher felt I could write," Stegner remembered. "He gave me good grades and patted me on the head and boosted

20. Stegner, *Bluebird*, 16.

21. Emphasis mine.

22. Stegner, *Bluebird*, 201.

23. Wallace Stegner, "Once in the Boy Scouts," in *Growing Up Western: Recollections of a Time Gone By*, ed. Clarus Backes (New York: Knopf, 1990).

24. Benson, *Wallace Stegner*, 44.

me out of freshman English at the end of the first quarter and into an advanced writing course with him." Fisher was an iconoclast who enjoyed taking a can opener to the unopened minds of what he called "Mormon provincials." He even organized a free-thinking Radical Club, which discussed such hot-button topics as birth control and the historicity of Jesus Christ—heady topics in 1927 Zion.[25]

Though nominally a secular institution, the U pulled a few punches at the intersection of theology and education. The anthropology department, for instance, cleaved to the teachings of the Book of Mormon. "I was taught that the Indians are the descendants of the Lost Tribes of Israel, and that they came up from South America as two tribes, the Nephites and the Lamanites," Stegner remembered. In that same class, he learned that "Jesus Christ left his footprints in Utah's Little Cottonwood Canyon when he visited North America—a detail that not even Mormon kids believed."[26]

Stegner grew an astonishing six inches during his senior year in high school, which opened the gates not only to the ROTC but also to sports. Overnight, the bookish weakling found himself playing freshman basketball and being rushed by a campus fraternity with a secret handshake and a book of tong songs. His reaction? "Beatitude."

Stegner never tired of thanking the U for granting him a fully rounded life. In the essay, "It Is the Love of Books That I Owe Them," he wrote:

> As my tennis-and-basketball-playing friends ushered me into the human world and taught me how to belong, this handful of teacher friends introduced me to the life of the mind where, even though I didn't know it then, I most wanted to live. No university, even the greatest, could have done much more.

Stegner called his college years "the happiest time of my life.... I came as a scared sixteen-year-old freshman into an expanding universe and for a while expanded with it." He experienced physical and personal growth, and "Along with growth, friends. There have been

25. Richard W. Etulain and Wallace Stegner, *Conversations with Wallace Stegner on Western History and Literature*, revised edition (Salt Lake City: University of Utah Press, 1990), 24, 25.

26. Etulain and Stegner, *Conversations*, 113.

no such friends since. . . . They were hearts of gold, and they accepted *me*. . . . I was happy as a shrimp in cocktail sauce."[27]

Stegner fell hard for Salt Lake City. He worked for a summer selling hot dogs and hamburgers at Saltair, the stately pleasure dome/resort on the western shore of the Great Salt Lake. And he rhapsodized about the smell of the geography, both in the fictional *Big Rock Candy Mountain*, "like no other smell on earth, a stink almost,"[28] and much later, in a 1983 memoir:

> In 1924, memory tells me, the lake air was hot, rich with the odors of popcorn, spun candy, and frying meat. The whole pavilion, even the potted palms, glittered with an airborne deposit of salt.[29]

In his 1979 novel, *Recapitulation*, Stegner-as-Bruce-Mason (the narrator of *The Big Rock Candy Mountain*, now an older, successful, globe-trotting diplomat) revisits his hometown and experiences a searing nostalgia:

> If there were a streetcar in sight now he would take it; any number, it wouldn't matter. . . . When he first came to Salt Lake City he had never seen a streetcar—had barely made the acquaintance of the water closet. The pure American frontier savage, with everything to learn about how people live in groups, he had ridden every line in town, just to see where it went.

When Stegner said he craved belonging, he meant it. "Simply by its public transportation, Salt Lake had opened the door to membership just when *he most needed something to belong to.* It served native and stranger, young and old, Gentile and Mormon, alike. It promoted the beginning of a wary confidence. He knew where he was and how to get somewhere else."[30]

Like the protagonist of *Recapitulation,* Stegner had to roam the world to discover where he came from. Writing about Salt Lake City in the essay "A Gentile in the New Jerusalem," Stegner commented, "I discover that much of my youth is there, and a surprising lot of

---

27. Robert Steensma, *Stegner in Salt Lake City* (Salt Lake City: University of Utah Press, 2007), 72.

28. Stegner, *Big Rock,* 388.

29. Wallace Stegner and Page Stegner, *American Places* (New York: Penguin Classics, 2006), 104.

30. Wallace Stegner, *Recapitulation* (New York: Doubleday, 1979), 75. Emphasis mine.

my heart. Having blown tumbleweed-fashion around the continent so that I am forced to *select* a hometown, I find myself selecting the City of the Saints, for what seems to me cause."

In the same essay, he elaborated,

> In Salt Lake I wrote my first short story and my first novel. In Salt Lake I fell in love for the first time and was rudely jilted for the first time and recovered for the first time. In Salt Lake I took my first drink and acquired a delightful familiarity with certain speakeasies that I could find now blindfolded if there were any necessity. I experimented with either beer and peach brandy and bathtub gin and survived them all.

"Wallace Stegner sought kindness," his friend and Sierra Club director Carl Pope observed, and "he found it in Zion." In Salt Lake, Stegner felt drowned "in acute recognitions." The city was founded as a place of refuge, he wrote, and it was "as sanctuary that it persists even in my Gentile mind and insinuates itself as my veritable hometown."[31]

31. Will Bagley, "'Except As a Friend': Wallace Stegner Among the Mormons," *Utah Historical Quarterly* 78, no. 2 (2010): 100–17.

TWO

Climbing the Mountain

"As I wrote some pages of it, I couldn't see the typewriter for tears."—Preface to *The Big Rock Candy Mountain*

After working his way through the University of Utah as a delivery boy and salesman for the I & M Rug and Linoleum Company, Stegner enrolled as a graduate student in American literature at the University of Iowa.

He chose an unusual subject for his Ph.D. thesis: the geologist and naturalist Clarence Edward Dutton, a nineteenth-century explorer who wrote early descriptions of five locales destined to become national parks—Yosemite, Yellowstone, Zion, Bryce, and the Grand Canyon. Dutton's connection to American literature was tenuous at best, but his connections to Clarence King of the U.S. Geological Survey (a peripheral character in Stegner's novel *Angle of Repose*) and to John Wesley Powell, whose biography Stegner would later write, were real. Stegner called his work a "very bad dissertation," but others disagreed. The University of Utah published the thesis as a book in 1936, and Jackson Benson admired it: "The dissertation shows its author, a young man of twenty-five, who . . . before environmentalism became the movement it is today, was concerned about preserving the beauties of the national parks and conserving our land heritage."[1]

After teaching for two years in graduate school, Stegner briefly commuted to the Swedish Lutheran Augustana College in Rock Island, Illinois, while finishing his doctorate in Iowa City. (Stegner

1. Jackson Benson, *Wallace Stegner: His Life and Work* (New York: Viking Penguin, 1996), 65, 66.

spent the academic year of 1932–1933 at the University of California, Berkeley, to be nearer his ailing mother in Los Angeles.) As a man who never evinced much interest in organized religion, Stegner sardonically recounted that he left the college "when a big fight broke out between the Evangelicals who had hired me and the Fundamentalists who thought dangerous latitudinarian standards were being followed." As an atheist, an agnostic, and a militant "nonbeliever in the Augsburg Confession"—a foundational document of the Lutheran church—Stegner had to go. In 1934, in the midst of the Great Depression, his former professors at the University of Utah summoned him back to Salt Lake City to teach in the English department.[2]

To-ing and fro-ing across the Great Plains, Stegner found time for romance. He fell for, wooed, and married a graduate student named Mary Page, a union that would last for fifty-nine years, the rest of his life. The nester had found his nest-mate. Neither husband nor wife ever claimed to be engaged in a literary partnership like that of, say, Vladimir and Vera Nabokov, but Stegner's marriage was a cornerstone of his existence. "Your best editor is your divorced wife," Wallace's daughter-in-law Lynn Stegner remembered him saying. "He wasn't divorced from her but . . . he wanted harsh criticism and he wanted strong criticism, candid criticism, and he always got that from Mary, and she was a good reader."[3]

In the last third of his life, Stegner became an avid defender of "old-fashioned" morality—he wrote a famous essay, "Born a Square"—and chafed out loud about the libertinism of the 1960s. There are no reports of infidelity, or even a hint of it , in the Stegner marriage.

Stegner's last few novels all celebrate the institution of marriage, or, in the case of *Angle of Repose*, impose a severe penalty for ignoring its strictures. "His most consistent subject is marriage, represented in a mode more epic than romantic," *New York Times* critic A. O. Scott wrote in a 2020 assessment of Stegner's legacy. "Monogamy, with its crags and chasms, is the most salient and imposing feature in his

2. Richard W. Etulain and Wallace Stegner, *Conversations with Wallace Stegner on Western History and Literature*, revised edition (Salt Lake City: University of Utah Press, 1990), 13 ff.

3. "Wallace Stegner," *PBS Utah*, aired July 2013, PBS Utah-KUED.

imaginative landscape, the human undertaking around which all the others are organized."[4]

Joe Alston, the fictional narrator of *All the Little Live Things* (1967) and *The Spectator Bird* (1976) grumbles in the latter novel: "These days people hesitate for a marriage license no longer than dogs in a vacant lot, and marriage vows, those quaint anachronisms, are about as binding as blue laws from the Code of Hammurabi." Describing *The Spectator Bird*, Benson calls Stegner "the balladeer of monogamy, a testifier to the experience of a marriage that has become exceedingly rare, a marriage—Joe's as well as Stegner's own—of nearly fifty years to the same person."[5]

When Wallace's son, Page, felt obliged to inform his father of his forthcoming divorce, he feared the moral condemnation of his forbidding-looking father.[6] He needn't have worried. Wallace said "he would support me in whatever I decided to do ... [then] embraced my new wife with open arms, loved her, and at the same time managed in some incredible kind and gentlemanly way to always remain a 'father-in-law' to my first wife."[7]

Stegner and Mary enjoyed life in Salt Lake City, much of it savored outdoors, but barely scraped by on his salary as an English instructor. Suddenly, a fortuitous break: Stegner, who had been writing short stories (publishing just two), spotted a posting for a novel-writing contest sponsored by the Boston publisher Little, Brown. He wanted to enter, but confessed to Mary that he didn't have any ideas for a novel. She told him a story she had heard in her family, about a doomed love triangle on the prairie. The kernel of Mary's idea sufficed. Stegner churned out the wonderful novella *Remembering Laughter*. Set on a remote Iowa farm, the superb prose of *Laughter* rubs up against the best of Willa Cather, no small achievement for a first-time novelist. In January 1937 he heard the news—he had won the contest.

The prize was $2,500, about $50,000 today. "In those days it was

4. A. O. Scott, "Wallace Stegner and the Conflicted Soul of the West," *The New York Times*, June 1, 2020.

5. Benson, *Wallace Stegner*, 174.

6. "His friends said he looked like God ought to look," wrote Timothy Egan in *The New York Times*, Feb. 18, 2009.

7. Benson, *Wallace Stegner*, 375.

a magnificent sum for a struggling English instructor, and we were, needless to say, overjoyed," Mary remembered. "Even though I was eight months pregnant, we decided to give a party. That night, after great celebration, I went into labor, and thirty hours later produced our only son, Page. Two great events in two days that changed our lives."[8]

To echo the title of Bernard DeVoto's masterwork about the nation's westward migrations, *The Year of Decision: 1846,* 1937 was a year of decision for Wallace Stegner. God bless them, he and Mary spent the *Laughter* proceeds unwisely, touring France and England on bicycles until the money started to run out. Whereupon Wallace headed off to the University of Wisconsin for yet another English instructorship. But more importantly, around Christmastime he started working on his *bildungsroman*, *The Big Rock Candy Mountain.*

Climbing the *Mountain* proved to be no easy task. Before its appearance in 1943, Stegner had published three interstitial novels, mainly to make a little money. *The Potter's House* (1938), *On a Darkling Plain* (1940), and *Fire and Ice* (1941) "were in one way or another experiments, and they were all to some extent failures," according to Benson. "For the most part, these early works are artificial, well-made but contrived."[9] Stegner basically agreed. He told Richard Etulain, "*On a Darkling Plain* embarrasses me. *Fire and Ice* rather embarrasses me, too, because it's politically naive in the same way that *On a Darkling Plain* is psychologically naive."

Benson calls the "novelette" *Fire and Ice* "the last of what might be called [Stegner's] apprenticeship fiction." (Stegner assured his agent that the book would be "utterly unsaleable.") *Kirkus Reviews*

---

8. Mary Page Stegner, foreword to *Remembering Laughter*, by Wallace Stegner (New York: Penguin Books, 1996). *Laughter* had more than one interesting backstory. One of the Little, Brown judges was Bernard DeVoto, and Stegner's routine thank-you note to the brilliant, sulfurous historian launched a lifelong friendship. Secondly, *Laughter*'s success precipitated a falling-out between Stegner and his mentor, the novelist Vardis Fisher. According to researcher Joseph Flora, "Fisher felt that *Remembering Laughter* (1937) was importantly indebted to his own work *Dark Bridwell* (1931)." In his 1970 essay "Vardis Fisher and Wallace Stegner: Teacher and Student," Flora points out some similarities between the two books, but concludes that Fisher simply envied *Laughter's* commercial success. Flora thinks Stegner took revenge by including a thinly veiled and unflattering portrait of Fisher in his short story "The View from the Balcony," as the hard-drinking, hawk-nosed psychiatry professor Paul Latour (Box 10, fd. 10, Wallace Stegner Papers, J. Willard Marriott Library, University of Utah, Salt Lake City).

9. Benson, *Wallace Stegner*, 83.

was unsparing:[10] One "had hoped that by now Stegner would have grown beyond the vignette type of book, but once again his story does not quite add up to a full-bodied novel. Facile, written with a hard, young style, he succeeds in leaving sharp impressions, without quite rounding out his theme."

Because Stegner never authorized new editions of these books, they have become valuable collectors' items. A copy of *Fire and Ice* now sells for $400. A good copy of *The Potter's House*, published by the Prairie Press of Muscatine, Iowa, now costs $1,800.

In 1938, a colleague from the Bread Loaf Writers Conference—at Middlebury College in Vermont, where Stegner had started teaching in the summer—nominated him for a Briggs-Copeland Fellowship at Harvard.[11] This would be yet another non-tenure-track position, teaching writing for only half a salary, but it would leave some time for him to work on *Mountain*. Plus, it was Harvard. Among his fellow Fellows were the future critic Mark Schorer and the famous, eccentric poet Delmore Schwartz, the model for Von Humboldt Fleischer in Saul Bellow's novel *Humboldt's Gift*.

The Utah-born DeVoto (of whom more later), an untenured professor in Harvard's history department, adopted the Stegners and introduced them into his circle, which included the economist John Kenneth Galbraith and historian Arthur Schlesinger, Jr. W. H. Auden would show up on campus. Americanists in the English department included F. O. Matthiessen and Perry Miller. One of the Briggs-Copeland writing students was named Norman Mailer. Harvard was *that* kind of place. "DeVoto, [Robert] Frost, Conrad Aiken and others made up a little community which hadn't existed anywhere I had lived up to that point," Stegner told Benson. "T. S. Eliot would come lecturing, and we would all go together."[12]

He wasn't in Iowa anymore.

For the family of three, money was a problem. "We were poor and motivated, hungry," Stegner told Etulain. "For thirty dollars I

10. *Kirkus Reviews*, Apr. 1, 1941.

11. Year of Decision, indeed. The summer Bread Loaf Writers Conference met in Middlebury, Vermont, and in his second year of teaching there, Stegner bought a second home and adjacent land in Greensboro, where he and Mary spent many summers until the end of their lives.

12. Benson, *Wallace Stegner*, 102.

would write anybody an article."[13] He summoned his inner beaver, churning out articles for *Publishers Weekly*, *Harper*'s (where DeVoto had solid connections), and *The Saturday Evening Post*. He wrote often for *The Delphian Quarterly*, prompting him to observe in later life that he wasn't exactly sure what *The Delphian Quarterly* was, but their checks cleared.[14]

Stegner never abandoned the Stakhanovite work ethic developed early in his career. He never hesitated to recycle material, and he made it clear that he wrote to make money, first and foremost. Biographer Philip Fradkin notes drolly that one of Stegner's first stories, published in *The Salt Lake Tribune*, later showed up in both *The Big Rock Candy Mountain* and *Wolf Willow*. He called Stegner "the king of recycling stories." Novelist Scott Turow, who was in the Stanford writing program, recalls commenting on an article Stegner had written while he was employed by the oil company ARAMCO. "He wasn't the least bit self-conscious about it," Turow recalled. "He viewed writing as a profession and he took the ARAMCO work as seriously as any other."

In 1943, the clouds parted. *The Big Rock Candy Mountain*, which Stegner had been working on for six years, appeared in September. In a 1974 preface to the novel, he called it "the first of my books to achieve wide recognition.... I see that it is also the most personal." "I wrote it because it happened to me," he explained, "the significance I found later. A lot of myself is invested in that book. As I wrote some pages of it, I couldn't see the typewriter for tears." When a colleague interrupted one of his classes at the Iowa Writers' Workshop in the summer of 1939 to tell him his father had died, his immediate response was: "Now I know how that damn book ends."[15]

The title, of course, refers to George Stegner's delirious faith in success, American style. "He was born with the itch in his veins, Elsa knew.... There was somewhere, if you knew where to find it, some place where money could be made like drawing water from a well, some Big Rock Candy Mountain where life was effortless and rich

13. Etulain and Stegner, *Conversations*, 45.

14. Benson, *Wallace Stegner*, 113.

15. Philip Fradkin, *Wallace Stegner and the American West* (New York: Alfred A. Knopf, 2008), 93.

and unrestricted and full of adventure and action, where something could be had for nothing."[16]

For a thirty-six-year-old novelist, *Mountain*'s success was a watershed moment. The reviews were not uniformly positive, but they appeared in prestigious publications across the country. The previously vitriolic *Kirkus Reviews* called it "one of the important novels of the Fall season," declaring that "this is the most important book Wallace Stegner has done, and he has been marked as 'a comer' ever since his memorable novelette, *Remembering Laughter*."[17]

The book received two reviews in *The New York Times*—in the daily newspaper and on Sunday—back when the *Times* still allowed this to happen. In the *Sunday Times Book Review*, critic Joseph Warren Beach wrote that

> Wallace Stegner's latest book shows great advance in power and grasp over the shorter novels for which he is chiefly known, and is a much more satisfying example of regional fiction.[18]

Ouch.

The *Times* would occasionally bedevil Stegner during his long career, and Beach's subsequent demurral set the tone for later slights. He prissily wrote that Stegner "somewhat misses that peculiar pleasure that is to be derived from a work of literary art." According to Beach, the young novelist's style and aesthetic sense were still in their formative stages.[19]

Beach was right; the prose of *Mountain* was workmanlike at best. Still, the novel has endured. If Stegner wrote it through teary eyes, he has moistened the eyes of thousands of readers in the eighty years since it appeared. He spares neither himself, nor the reader, any family heartache. The story of the striver Bo Mason, his unhappy wife, Elsa, and their two sons is grandiose, ambitious, and tragic. Bo's older brother's youthful, unexpected death—a precise reenactment of Stegner's brother Cecil's early passing—his father's descent into

16. Wallace Stegner, *Big Rock Candy Mountain*, revised edition (New York: Penguin Classics, 2010), 83.

17. *Kirkus Reviews*, Sep. 1, 1943.

18. Ouch!

19. Joseph Warren Beach, "Life-Size Stegner," *The New York Times*, Sep. 26, 1943.

alcoholism and self-destruction, and his mother's desperate flights to local sanatoria are all manifest in the novel.

His mother's last words—"Which . . . way?"—are delicately placed on the dying lips of Elsa Mason.

Now the peripatetic Stegner prepared to make his final move. He had never been particularly happy at Harvard, which had no plans to grant him or his friend DeVoto tenure. "When I was teaching at Harvard," Stegner wrote in the essay "Growing Up Western," "which should have been my highest ambition, I found that I couldn't wait to get back west." By way of scratching his Western itch, he researched and published his informal history *Mormon Country* during his last year at Harvard, and—again through the intervention of a Bread Loaf colleague— received the job offer of a lifetime. In 1944, Edith Mirrielees recommended him as her successor as a creative writing teacher at Stanford. The university acquiesced, offering Stegner a tenured professorship with a half-time teaching load.[20] Stegner later said he leapt at the Stanford job "like a nine-inch trout on a copper trolling line."[21]

"After several years of graduate school in Iowa and California and a decade of teaching in Illinois, Utah, Wisconsin and Massachusetts," Stegner recalled, "I arrived with my wife and son at Stanford and the house in the Coast Range foothills, within sight of the last sunsets on the continent, where we have lived ever since."[22]

20. Benson, *Wallace Stegner*, 151.
21. Etulain and Stegner, *Conversations*, 14.
22. "Growing Up Western," typescript, box 141, fd. 2, Wallace Stegner Papers.

THREE

A Not Unfriendly Alliance

"I could never write about them ... except as a friend." —Wallace Stegner, on the Mormons[1]

Chronology is the enemy of biography, meaning that the events in one's life don't always seem to occur where they should. It is crazy, for instance, that Stegner published three short, not exactly top-quality, novels during the same six-year period that he was working on *The Big Rock Candy Mountain*. It is equally inconvenient for my reconstruction of Stegner's life that, one year before he published *Mountain*, he finished his first fascinating sally into Western history, *Mormon Country*.

"In Cambridge I wrote, out of sheer nostalgia, the nonfiction book *Mormon Country*," Stegner explained, "and when that was done I sat down seriously to the events that had mattered to me, and finished *The Big Rock Candy Mountain*." "What I was homesick for was not merely Salt Lake," he elaborated in the essay "Growing Up Western,"

> a city in a valley between mountains, with the glint of the lake off westward, but for a whole region, a whole lifetime of acclimatization and expectation.... It was the whole West, and I began to realize how much it had to do in the making of me.

Mormon Country was part of the American Folkways series of books edited by the novelist Erskine Caldwell (*Tobacco Road*). He commissioned books on parts of America defined by "folkways,"

1. Wallace Stegner, "Finding the Place: A Migrant Childhood," in *Where the Bluebird Sings to the Lemonade Springs: Living and Writing in the West,* reprint edition (New York: Random House Publishing Group, 2002), 16.

not geography. "The colorful story of American life is here being told for the first time through its own galvanic medium[!]", Caldwell wrote of the series. "Professing no kinship whatsoever to the school of glorified road maps and esoteric lore, this series examines the habits of thought and behavior of Americans from the point of view of the men and women who propagated the national culture."[2] He ultimately edited twenty-five books in the twenty-eight-volume series, including Carey McWilliams's groundbreaking work on the creation of greater Los Angeles: *Southern California: An Island on the Land.*

Stegner knew better than most that the "folkways" of Mormonism extended well beyond Utah. He appreciated the sprawl of Brigham Young's Deseret empire throughout the Intermountain West, and if he didn't use a phrase like "Mormon Culture Zone," he certainly thought in those terms. The book's original flyleaf correctly noted that Mormon Country "includes all of Utah, most of southern Idaho, the southwest corner of Wyoming, much of Arizona and Nevada, and strips of Colorado and New Mexico. It was an arid and inhospitable land until the Mormons transformed its wilderness reaches into a secure haven."

Stegner's field notes for the book reveal a granular knowledge of the landscape he is writing about. As illustrations for the book, he suggests:

> Black Hawk Encampment, Heber City, July 15–19, and Wasatch County Fair. Get esp. the square stone houses and the frequent hotpots, private natural swimming pools, in yards; sometimes dead hotpots [sic] utilized as root cellars. This one of the best Mormon towns, most pictorial.

And:

> At Farson, on the Little Sandy, two markers commemorate the Sandy Pony Express system & Brigham's meeting with Bridger. East on Wyo 28 to South Pass—Plenty antelope—Wind Rivers long and [illegible] to the north.

2. William Stegner, *Mormon Country* (New York: Duell, Sloan & Pearce, 1942), back jacket.

His notes also include thumbnail biographies of his characters, e.g., "Brigham—Golden-haired & blue eyed, round faced, stout, later pudgy, affable & approachable, but could cloud up when crossed."[3]

Mormon Country is the first published expression of Stegner's fondness for the Mormons. (He did compare a priapic rooster to Brigham Young in *Remembering Laughter.*) Early in the book, he hails "the Mutual," the Mutual Improvement Association where he spent so many of his adolescent evenings in the basements of Salt Lake City ward houses, dancing, acting, or playing basketball. While he notes that the adults present kept a close lid on teen hijinks, particularly smoking, "Mutual is fun. . . .

> The Church has never objected to social activities like music and dancing and the theater. Brigham Young guessed publicly that there was a lot more singing and dancing in Heaven than in Hell, and he saw no reason why the Saints should try to imitate the hot place. Mormons have always been a singing and dancing and sociable people. So long as the fun is socially acceptable and decorous, the Church approves.[4]

Growing up, Stegner had a tumultuous family life, and he was grateful that the Latter-day Saints had operated *in loco parentis* for him during his adolescence. As he told Richard Etulain many years later, "These people were so confident of their family life that they just threw open the doors in every direction. It wasn't a desperation move . . . but part of living their religion. The family is so important in Mormon religion that without it the religion would hardly exist."[5]

Mormon Country is an unbuckled outing, difficult to categorize. It starts out with a short fictional vignette, "Meet Me at the Ward House," and includes many diverting, short biographies of such characters as John Wesley Powell, Earl Douglass, Everett Reuss, and Butch Cassidy (né George LeRoy Parker, whom Stegner insists was born a Mormon). The book contains plenty of autobiography, including Stegner's unexpected revelation that, for money, "I assisted

3. Field notes for *Mormon Country*, box 74, fd. 3, Wallace Stegner Papers, J. Willard Marriott Library, University of Utah, Salt Lake City.

4. Stegner, *Mormon Country*, 18.

5. Richard W. Etulain and Wallace Stegner, *Conversations with Wallace Stegner on Western History and Literature*, revised edition (Salt Lake City: University of Utah Press, 1990), 102.

a good Saint in the writing of a book designed to promote faith and a reverence for the home and family among the Mormon people." That book was called "The Home Evening Hour," the purpose of which, he wrote, "was to bind the family together by promoting religion, education and recreation in an informal gathering in the home one evening a week." He correctly viewed the weekly family gathering as the observant Mormon family's companion to the Mutual Improvement Association, "and like the M.I.A., it is a source of strength."[6]

Stegner wrote that the Mormon settlers were better stewards of Western lands than any other pioneer or settler group. Their communitarian values, he argued, were ideally suited to the taming and proper exploitation—"wise use" might be a more modern term—of the arid, mountainous lands.

"By revelation and accident and adaptation the Mormons discovered what the cliff-dwellers had discovered centuries before," Stegner wrote, "that the only way to be a farmer in the Great Basin and on the desert plateaus of the Colorado watershed was to be a group farmer." He likened Mormon villages to Pueblo and Zuni settlements; "The pattern is not the usual American pattern; in many ways the life and the institutions it has produced are unique."[7]

Stegner would make it his Miltonic life task to justify the ways of Mormons to man—meaning non-believers—whom the Saints call "gentiles."

The counterpoint to the Mormons' wise use policies, according to Stegner, was Bo Mason's frenetic search for a figurative El Dorado, a world "where something could be had for nothing." The mantra of the gentile settlers, Stegner believed, was "get in, get rich, get out. It's always been a treasure hunt—and never a settlement."

At times, *Mormon Country* waxes rhapsodic about the Latter-day Saints. Stegner loves the "Mormon trees," i.e. the Lombardy poplar, and he is hardly the first writer to compare the Saints' westward trek to the flight of the children of Israel:

> They had found their strength: Mormonism in exodus was a herd, like a

6. Stegner, *Mormon Country,* 174–75.
7. Stegner, *Mormon Country,* 30, 31.

herd of buffalo, and its strength was the herd strength and the cunning of the tough old bulls who ran the show. Brigham Young was no seer and revelator, but a practical leader, an organizer and colonizer of very great stature.[8]

Stegner admired Brigham for some of his less salutary qualities: "Throughout his career Brigham . . . fanned the hatred of the Gentiles, he fostered the sense of being surrounded and persecuted." "He held his aces back to back," Stegner wrote, "and he opened strong and kept raising, to freeze out the grocery clerks. . . . There were few grocery clerks among the Mormon pioneers."[9]

For a non-Mormon, Stegner offers up a pretty orthodox account of the 1856 handcart tragedy, during which more than two hundred pioneers, most of them pushing their effects across the mountains in flimsy, two-wheeled carts, died trying to reach Salt Lake City. After noting the lucky ones who made it "home" into the Wasatch Valley, Stegner suggests that "the uncounted dead who lay along the trail (one Church historian estimates the number of casualties at one hundred forty-five out of five hundred eighty) were home, too." They "could rest in the assurance that their sacrifices had sanctified them in the eyes of the Most High."[10]

So what did the studiously areligious Stegner ("About God I simply do not know; I don't think I can know"[11]), who couldn't be bothered to read the Augsburg Confession to save his teaching job, think of Joseph Smith's religion? Not much. In a nutshell, Stegner admired everything about the Mormons—their morals, their (yes) beaverishness, their collective intelligence—except their religion.

His religious critique wasn't exactly consistent. In *Mormon Country*, he claims "the exorcism of devils was commonplace among the Mormons for fifty years and are by no means extinct even today," meaning in 1942. He likewise noted the belief in "second sight," the penchant for speaking in tongues and the presence of "water-witches" and "walkers-after-death" among the Saints. "Mormonism," Stegner writes,

8. Stegner, *Mormon Country*, 60.
9. Stegner, *Mormon Country*, 61.
10. Stegner, *Mormon Country*, 83.
11. Will Bagley, "'Except As a Friend': Wallace Stegner Among the Mormons," *Utah Historical Quarterly* 78, no. 2 (2010): 108.

> is shot through with a theology that to outsiders looks like the wildest superstition, and a superstition that has almost become a theology. It is a composite and complicated web, product of the ignorance and witchcraft of the frontier, the pseudo-science of amateur anthropologists and sociologists, the ignorance and superstition of the under-privileged people of Europe who became converts.[12]

But then, a couple of hundred pages later, Stegner calls Mormonism "a practical religion, dedicated to the affairs of the world as a preparation for the material resurrection into the millennium." "Unorthodox as much of its theological and social experimentation has been, it never lost its hold on the things of this earth," he writes. "It has always been at bottom, among the people."[13]

While preparing *Mormon Country*, Stegner had a fascinating exchange with historian and researcher Dale Morgan, who counseled him about Mormon history and folkways. Stegner told Morgan that he saw traits in Mormon history—a private army, a secret police, esoteric symbols, an "encirclement myth"—that reminded him of the totalitarian regimes in Germany and Japan. But Morgan pushed back; he "was more protective of the faith of his fathers than his faithful critics give him credit," said historian Will Bagley, who unearthed the exchange.

> [Morgan] pointed to what Stegner called territorial dynamism and "the psychology of dispossession" combined with "a frontal attack by a society upon an environment. The whole Mormon experience with the land must be taken into consideration in any dissection of Mormon society—this is part of what I mean by inferring the intervention of the frontier."[14]

Mormon Country would be Stegner's first book to be reviewed in *The New York Times*, and quite favorably: "His book makes excellent reading and is solidly based." Reviewer George Stewart sardonically noted that Stegner's forthright and disapproving remarks about polygamy ("Polygamy is dead but its soul is marching on") are "not likely to improve his sales under the shadow of the Wasatch."[15] The

12. *Mormon Country,* 153–54.
13. *Mormon Country,* 343.
14. Bagley, "Except As a Friend," 110.
15. George B. Stewart, "Land of the Mormons," *The New York Times*, Oct. 25, 1942.

Chicago Sun and *Boston Globe* reviewed the book, and *The Salt Lake Tribune* published a rave review under the headline "One-time Utah Educator Writes Superb 'Biography' of Region and People of *Mormon Country*."

In a 1977 book on Stegner, co-authors Forrest and Margaret Robinson accused him of going too easy on the Saints. Specifically, Stegner soft-pedaled polygamy, they wrote. (To be fair, the church had renounced plural marriage fifty years before Stegner's book appeared.) "We hear nothing of the Saints' racism," they continued, "and too little of the lusterless drudgery that was the portion of most Mormon women. It may be that Stegner's version of Mormon despotism is a trifle on the benevolent side."[16]

To his credit, Stegner knew what he thought about the Mormons, and he hardly wavered from his early, warm assessment of their society. "It would be fatal to generalize" about Mormonism, he wrote in *Mormon Country*, although that is something he did quite often. He did acknowledge the church's "share of bigots, parochial intolerants, and authoritarians." And he accused the Saints' patriarchy of keeping women "in their place as cooks, housekeepers, and breeding machines."

But "it is just as true to say that among garden-variety Saints one finds rather more human kindness, more neighborliness, more willingness to devote time and trouble to the assistance of their fellows, than one will find in most sections of the United States."[17]

In the 1979 novel *Recapitulation,* the Stegner stand-in, Bruce Mason, recalls feeling like an "impostor" while attending a Mormon wedding:

> He knows that every single aspect of his background, if it were known, would be a black mark against him, and their solidarity makes him half envious. He feels how satisfying it would be to belong to some tribe or family, and though he feels superior to this one, he does not dismiss the notion of *a not unfriendly alliance.*[18]

"I was never tempted to adopt [the Mormons'] beliefs," Stegner

16. Jackson Benson, *Wallace Stegner: His Life and Work* (New York: Viking Penguin, 1996), 123.

17. Stegner, *Mormon Country,* 187–88.

18. Emphasis mine.

wrote. "But I could never write about them, when it came to that, except as a friend."[19]

19. Wallace Stegner, "Finding the Place: A Migrant Childhood," in *Bluebird.*

FOUR

Biographies of the West

"Benny was loaded."
—Wallace Stegner in an interview with Gretchen Shoff

As a writer and commentator, Wallace Stegner embraced the West. As writing teachers tirelessly (and again, tiresomely) emphasize: He wrote about what he knew. He was self-conscious about his affinity for the West, and, like many Western writers, occasionally lashed out at the literary establishment's perceived pro-East Coast bias. John Steinbeck, too, railed against the cultural hegemony of the East Coast literary elite, and he won the Nobel Prize. What on earth was he complaining about?

Stegner had a proprietary definition of the West. His territory started west of the 100th meridian, basically where America starts to get dry. The Gulf of Mexico's rain shadow provides some moisture for the Great Plains but does not extend beyond the eastern border of the Texas panhandle. Describing the 100th meridian for *Century* magazine in 1890, the explorer/geographer/cartographer John Wesley Powell (one of Stegner's heroes) wrote:

> On the east a luxuriant growth of grass is seen, and the gaudy flowers of the order *Compositae* make the prairie landscape beautiful. Passing westward, species after species of luxuriant grass and brilliant flowering plants disappear; *the ground gradually becomes naked*, with "bunch" grasses here and there; now and then a thorny cactus is seen, and the yucca plant thrusts out its sharp bayonets. At the western margin of the zone the arid lands proper are reached.[1]

1. J. W. Powell, "Institutions for the Arid Lands," *The Century Magazine*, May 1890, 111–16. Emphasis mine.

In his 1964 account of the Mormon Trek, Stegner notes that the Saints' "crossing of the Loup Fork [in Nebraska] was almost directly on the 98th meridian, *that all-but-mystical line* at which begins another climate, another flora and fauna, another ecology, another light, another palette, another air, *another order of being*." Crossing that line, he writes, the Mormons have entered "the incontrovertible West," where the buffalo chips are dry, not wet, and if you want water, you are going to have to dig for it.[2]

Stegner's admittedly idiosyncratic West extended to the Sierra Nevada and excluded California, the Pacific Northwest, and much of the Southwest. He dismissed California as "a nation of in-migrants, and its writers are in-migrants, too, either writing about the places they came from or frantically scratching around and reading 'Sunset' [magazine] to find specifically Californian patterns to which to conform."[3] More reasonably, he called the Southwest "historically and ethnically another country."

The land west of the Sierra and the northern coastal range was just too verdant, too darned easy to live in, to interest Stegner. The arid lands fascinated him, one, because he came of age in Utah, and two, because he felt, counterintuitively, that they were arguably America's real heartland, the geography that made or broke the toughest settlers. Stegner's West was "a land of little rain and big consequences."[4]

On some level, Stegner felt that people like the Harvard historian Henry Adams and his Yale-educated friend Clarence King, the first director of the U.S. Geological Survey—both of whom were minor characters in the novel *Angle of Repose*—were East Coast swells who chattered about the West but ultimately weren't up to the task of taming it. "To grow up with the West, or to grow with and through it into national prominence, you had to have the West bred in your bones, *you needed it facing you like a dare*."[5]

He deemed his West to be fragile, unlike, say, Vermont. "You can

---

2. Wallace Stegner, *The Gathering of Zion: The Story of the Mormon Trail* (Lincoln, NB and London: University of Nebraska Press, 1981), 129. Emphasis mine.

3. Wallace Stegner, "Born a Square," in *The Sound of Mountain Water: The Changing American West* (New York: Vintage, 2017), 171.

4. Jackson Benson, *Wallace Stegner: His Life and Work* (New York: Viking Penguin, 1996), 242.

5. Benson, *Wallace Stegner*, 217. Emphasis mine.

tear the hell out of Vermont woods and pretty soon, five years, you can't tell that the loggers have been in there," he wrote. "But you can't do that in the West."[6] And he inveighed endlessly against the improper exploitation of the dry lands by get-rich-quick hustlers of the Bo Mason ilk:

> The history of the West until recently has been a history of the importation of humid-land habits (and carelessnesses) into a dry land that will not tolerate them; and of the indulgence of an unprecedented personal liberty, an atomic individualism, in a country that experience says can only be successfully tamed and lived in by a high degree of cooperation.[7]

As mentioned, Stegner revered the Mormons as the model husbandmen of the arid lands because they were "stickers," they came to live on the land, not exploit it and move on. "These whiskered zealots," he wrote, cherished "a group dream, not an individual one; a dream of Millennium, not of quick fortune."[8] It was as if they had read Stegner's yet-to-be-written tomes about the West.

"The Mormon village is a green village," he wrote in *Mormon Country*. "It was unthinkable that the gathering place of the Saints should be a barren desert. It should be made to blossom and it was." Stegner loved that Brigham Young encouraged women to carry rose cuttings, geranium slips, and seedling trees on the seemingly endless trek. He lauded "the characteristic marks of Mormon settlement: the typical, intensively cultivated fields of alfalfa and sugar beets and Bermuda onions and celery, the orchards of cherry and apple and peach and apricot."[9]

Stegner viewed the fate of the West in profoundly moral terms. Decades after he wrote his first book about the Mormons, he memorably coined the term "geography of hope" to describe his faith in the arid lands. "Angry as one may be at what heedless men have done and still do to a noble habitat, one cannot be pessimistic about

6. Richard W. Etulain and Wallace Stegner, *Conversations with Wallace Stegner on Western History and Literature*, revised edition (Salt Lake City: University of Utah Press, 1990), 147.

7. Wallace Stegner, *Beyond the Hundredth Meridian: John Wesley Powell and the Second Opening of the West* (New York: Penguin, 1992), 362.

8. William Stegner, *Mormon Country* (New York: Duell, Sloan & Pearce, 1942), 62.

9. Stegner, *Mormon Country*, 21, 29.

the West," he insisted. "When it fully learns that cooperation, not rugged individualism, is the quality that most characterizes and preserves it, then it will have achieved itself and outlived its origins."[10]

Stegner wrote only two biographies, if you don't count his quickie Ph.D. thesis (a forty-page book) on Clarence Dutton. They were both of men he unreservedly admired: the historian Bernard DeVoto and John Wesley Powell. They were very different characters, hailing from different eras. But they earned Stegner's undying respect because they "got" the West, meaning their views on the proper exploitation of the lands between the mountains aligned closely with his own.

In retrospect, it might seem impossible that Stegner and DeVoto would not become friends, even if DeVoto hadn't surfaced on the Little, Brown prize committee that changed Stegner's life. DeVoto's story closely paralleled Stegner's. Born and educated in Ogden, Utah, DeVoto knew the "folkways" of the Beehive State just as intimately as Stegner did, although he appreciated them far less. In an oral history interview, Stegner remarked sardonically that "I actually knew Utah a whole lot better than Benny did, because he grew up without an automobile, and I grew up with one.... He hardly ever got out of Ogden, but I was all over the state."[11]

Stegner and DeVoto also had the Mormons in common. Stegner favored the Saints; DeVoto had mixed feelings about them on a good day. DeVoto's father, Florian, was a serious Catholic, while his mother was a backslid "Jack Mormon." As Stegner explained it: "His mother was a Mormon and not a very good one."[12] Stegner liked his Mormons backslid. In a hilarious passage from *Mormon Country*, he described a Latter-day Saint elder vacationing at his cabin on the Fish Lake Plateau in southern Utah. Stegner wrote that while the elder was stacking wood at the back of the cabin, unnoticed, the patriarch

> yawned like the tabernacle pipe organ. Then he went to the corner of the back porch, reached under it, and pulled out a jug. He contemplated it lovingly, rubbing the glassy shoulder, then tipped it and gurgled a long

10. Wallace Stegner, introduction to *Mountain Water*, 29.

11. Wallace Stegner, "The Artist as Environmental Advocate," an oral history conducted in 1982 by Ann Lage, Sierra Club History Series, Regional Oral History Office, The Bancroft Library, University of California, Berkeley. https://digitalassets.lib.berkeley.edu/roho/ucb/text/stegner_wallace.pdf, p. 60.

12. Etulain and Stegner, *Conversations*, 109.

time. When he brought it down again his eyes were clearer and he saw me. He cackled, "By golly," he said, "that's the way I like to fish."[13]

DeVoto's father was a "bitter anti-Mormon," Stegner recalled, and his son "joined him among Mormonism's sworn enemies." DeVoto wrote some unflattering words about Mormonism's founder Joseph Smith, whom he called "that poor crazed man." "[Smith] had always been drunk on glory," DeVoto wrote, "now he was drunk on power." Like Stegner, however, DeVoto admired Brigham Young, whom he considered one of the heroes of the nineteenth century.[14] Young, per DeVoto, was "one of the foremost intelligences of the times, the first American who learned how to colonize the desert."

Mimicking Stegner, DeVoto admired the Saints' collectivist ethos in settling the West. Stegner credited his friend with the wry observation "that the only true individualists in the West generally wound up at the end of a rope whose other end was in the hands of a bunch of cooperating citizens."[15]

Stegner's lines about DeVoto could very well apply to himself: "He was never a believer; to the end of his life he refused to take Mormon doctrines seriously. But he learned to take the Mormon people and Mormon virtues seriously, and to respect them, and it troubled him all his life that he was hated in his home state."

DeVoto *was* hated in Utah, and he came by it honestly. He viciously lampooned Ogden in his first novel, *The Crooked Mile*, and then, at the behest of H. L. Mencken, roasted the entire state in a 1926 essay simply titled "Utah." "Civilized life does not exist in Utah," DeVoto wrote from the comfort of a professorship at Northwestern University. "There people talk of only the Prophet, hogs and Fords."

DeVoto kissed off sixty years of hostility between the Mormons ("pious cowherds who believed themselves capable of summoning angels to converse with them") and gentiles (the "unfit of the frontier") then laid into the "utter mediocrity of life in the new Utah," a "commonwealth of greengrocers who have lifted themselves from the peasantry." "How do people live in Utah?" DeVoto concluded.

---

13. Stegner, *Mormon Country*, 189.

14. Wallace Stegner, *The Uneasy Chair: A Biography of Bernard DeVoto* (New York: Doubleday, 1974), 478.

15. Etulain and Stegner, *Conversations*, 149.

"They join the businessmen's calisthenics class at the gymnasium. Or they buy Fords on the five-dollar-a-week basis. Or they yawn. Or they die."

Stegner claimed that he was walking past a history professor's door at the University of Utah in 1927 when a copy of *The American Mercury* came flying out of the office and down the hall. It proved to be the issue with DeVoto's inflammatory attack on Utah. Stegner read the article and savored its "happy vehemence." "If he got a few innocent bystanders," Stegner later wrote, "I was willing to sacrifice them for the pleasure of looking at the more deserving corpses."[16]

Where Stegner was reasonable and pacific, DeVoto was stormy; the opposites attracted. Jackson Benson thinks DeVoto's cussedness may have cost his friend a Pulitzer Prize. In his introduction to *Beyond the Hundredth Meridian,* DeVoto performed a gratuitous drive-by on *The Growth of American Thought*, by Merle Curti, winner of the 1944 Pulitzer for history. DeVoto wrote that Curti "approached the West with a handful of cliches." Curti, an eminent academic historian, sat on the Pulitzer jury for history in 1954, the year Stegner's Powell biography—arguably his finest work of non-fiction—appeared. Benson reports that Stegner's biography made the final cut, but lost the prize because of DeVoto's shenanigans: "This was a lesson in moderation to a man already inclined to moderation."[17]

Stegner called DeVoto "a total maverick"[18] with an "incomparable knack of infuriating people." "He despised literary phonies, narcissistic artists, public confessors, gushers, long-hairs, and writers of deathless prose; and he would despise these because he feared them in himself."

DeVoto found his way to Harvard as an undergraduate and stayed there most of his life, first as a graduate student and then as a distinguished, but untenured, instructor in the history department. The Harvard historian Arthur Schlesinger, Jr., observed that the DeVoto and Stegner families had more than just Utah in common. During Prohibition, DeVoto was a rumrunner, just like George Stegner!

16. David Rich Lewis, "Bernard DeVoto's 'Utah;' History and Criticism from a Native Son," *Salt Lake Magazine*, January/February 2000.

17. Benson, *Wallace Stegner,* 224.

18. Benson, *Wallace Stegner*, 262.

"After forays in Canada," Schlesinger recalled, "he used to drive up to our back door and deliver carefully wrapped packages that turned out to contain bottles of whiskey and gin."[19]

When Stegner arrived in Cambridge on his Briggs-Copeland fellowship, DeVoto took him under his wing. ("During his Harvard years, Stegner continued to absorb technique, subject matter, and alcohol from DeVoto," writes Fradkin.) They played badminton together and discussed faculty politics. DeVoto, twelve years Stegner's senior, offered professional advice. Some of it didn't click. For instance, when DeVoto offered to share his files of hack fiction—in his case, often written under a pseudonym—to help Stegner make money. "I could never write to a formula," Stegner later said, "but I thought that was decent of him."[20]

More significantly, Stegner felt that DeVoto taught him how to write sparkling, factual history, the kind of history that people wanted to read. "Stegner's concept of how history should be written would seem to be almost entirely formed in his discussions with DeVoto,"[21] Benson thought. DeVoto, in turn, was a disciple of Francis Parkman, one of the first serious historians of the American West. Parkman aspired to "paint the forest in true and vivid colors" and espoused an approach of "history as synecdoche,"[22] meaning telling individuals' stories as shorthand for their times. In his 1884 classic, *Montcalm and Wolfe*, Parkman explained that "the names on the titlepage stand as representative of the two nations whose final contest for the control of North America is the subject of the book."[23]

Stegner adored DeVoto's famous trilogy of Western history, *The Year of Decision: 1846*, *Across the Wide Missouri*, and *The Course of Empire*, in part because he saw them as manifestations of DeVoto's personal acquaintance with the "weather, landscape and coloring and quality of light, drouth and distance" of the West. Stegner praised the books' "quality of personal participation, *in the way history can be*

19. Bernard DeVoto, *The Year of Decision 1846* (Boston, MA: Little, Brown, 1943), xvii.

20. Etulain and Stegner, *Conversations*, 29.

21. Benson, *Wallace Stegner*, 120.

22. Benson, *Wallace Stegner*, 121.

23. James Tuttleton, "Simon Schama, Francis Parkman, and the Writing of History," *New Criterion* 10, no. 1 (Sep. 1991), 39.

felt on the skin and in the muscles because the author himself has been able to imagine it that way, having taken the trouble to live as much of it as possible himself."[24]

Stegner was quick to acknowledge DeVoto's help in fashioning his own view of the West. In 1986, an interviewer marveled at the eleven years Stegner spent working on his John Wesley Powell biography, which she called "a masterwork of dazzling virtuosity, weaving together history, geography, biology, geology."

"How did you know what questions to ask yourself, or where to look for answers?" she asked.

"Whenever I needed to know what to do next, I'd ask Benny," Stegner answered. "Benny knew everything about the West. Benny was loaded."[25]

DeVoto's letters of "encouragement" to Stegner, laboring on the Powell book, are hilarious. Writing about Powell is "easy, my boy," DeVoto insisted, "it's just looking at maps for ten years. Oh, and being wrong about them."

In 1974, Stegner published *The Uneasy Chair: A Biography of Bernard DeVoto* nineteen years after his friend had died at age fifty-eight. This was an extraordinary act of friendship and devotion; the world was hardly clamoring to read DeVoto's life story, especially so long after his death. The title refers to the *Harper*'s magazine column "The Easy Chair," which DeVoto wrote for twenty years.

Stegner's biography is erudite, loving, and evenhanded. "I didn't want to leave out his warts, because he was all warts," Stegner said.[26] He called out his friend's vituperative personality when appropriate, and, perhaps painfully, he pulled no punches on DeVoto's flounderings as a fiction writer. "He knew he wrote novels badly," Stegner wrote.[27] Taking note of DeVoto's four novels penned under the pseudonym John August, Stegner observed, "These are all honest

---

24. Wallace Stegner, introduction to *The Course of Empire*, by Bernard DeVoto (New York: Houghton Mifflin, 1998). Emphasis added.

25. Gretchen Holstein Shoff, "Where the Bluebird Sings: Remembering Wallace Stegner," *Wisconsin Academy Review* (Winter 93–94): 19–23.

26. James Hepworth, *Stealing Glances: Three Interviews with Wallace Stegner* (Albuquerque, N.M.: University of New Mexico Press, 1998), 72.

27. Wallace Stegner, *The Uneasy Chair* (Lincoln, NE: University of Nebraska Press, 2001), 171.

books and competent ones.... But for me at least the thrill of life is not in them."[28] "It is as if [DeVoto] trusted history but he didn't trust his own imagination, quite." Stegner remarked to Etulain.[29]

But by the time *The Uneasy Chair* appeared, the student had supplanted the master. Stegner knew how hard it was to make money writing, and he definitely performed work-for-hire, e.g., his "book," *Discovery! The Search for Arabian Oil*, serialized in ARAMCO's in-house magazine. But, unlike DeVoto, he had mastered the art of shifting seamlessly from narrative history to fiction. The book he published just before the DeVoto biography, *Angle of Repose*, won the 1971 Pulitzer Prize for fiction.

A perfect example of "history by synecdoche" would be Stegner's memorable biography of the one-armed explorer, geologist, cartographer, and bureaucratic infighter John Wesley Powell, whose pioneering treks led to the creation of the U.S. Geological Survey. In writing about Powell's adventures in the great river canyons of the arid lands, Stegner told the story he cared most about—the "second opening" and proper exploitation of the Intermountain West.

Powell was one hell of a character. He lost his arm at the Civil War battle of Shiloh, then led a series of Indiana-Jones-like expeditions on the Green and Colorado rivers, navigating all the great canyons, some of which he first named, e.g., Glen Canyon. Twice, Powell found himself dangling by one arm in his underwear over a raging torrent. That was called getting "rimmed."[30] On one astonishing trip to Indian country, as it was called in 1870 (the Battle of the Little Bighorn was still six years in the future) Powell joined forces with the famous Mormon pathfinder Jacob Hamblin to try to learn why Shivwits tribesmen had killed three of Powell's party the previous year. Powell never carried a weapon among Native Americans, and between them, he and Hamblin, one of whose wives was a Paiute, knew several local languages.

When the Shivwits showed up to treat with Ka-pur-ats ("One-Arm-Off"), the principals smoked pipes while the Indians explained that Powell's men had been mistaken for some frontiersmen who

28. Stegner, *Mountain Water*, 244.

29. Etulain and Stegner, *Conversations*, 158.

30. Stegner, *Beyond the Hundredth Meridian*, 72, 102.

had molested a squaw. Powell and Hamblin acknowledged the mistaken identity, spent the night with the Shivwits, and then went their separate way. Powell and Hamblin believed "that one who meant no harm could travel freely among Indians," and Stegner notes that Powell "always spoke with a straight tongue."[31]

Powell's core belief, promulgated from his perches at the Bureau of Ethology and the Geological Survey, was that the land west of the hundredth meridian was too dry for serious farming and there wasn't much anyone could do about it. "He looked at the Arid Region and saw neither desert nor garden," Stegner wrote. Speaking to the 1893 Irrigation Congress in Los Angeles, Powell "warned the delegates that there was only water for about twenty per cent of the land in the entire West. You can't make it; you can only hold it back and store it.... Aridity is something that you simply cannot fake out."[32]

Powell thought that most of the arid lands weren't worth cultivating, but where husbandry might work, he proposed "a revolution in the land laws." Instead of selling homestead tracts in cookie-cutter rectangles, he had the idea of dividing up the West by "coherent river basins and drainage basins."[33] "Powell proposed surveys based on the topography, letting farms be as irregular as they had to be to give everyone a water frontage and a patch of irrigable soil,"[34] Stegner wrote, with the aim of forestalling water monopolies and subsequent range wars.

For example, Powell floated the idea of re-mapping the counties of Montana so that borders would be defined by hydrographic basins rather than by arbitrary political lines.[35] Of course, this idea went nowhere. Montana did what it always did, with "county seats competitively chosen in the atmosphere of deal, coup and horse-trade."[36]

The prevailing view among the Western politicians in Congress was that "water follows the plow." How, no one could really explain. When Powell went to Capitol Hill to seek additional funding for his irrigation surveys, Western Congressmen cut him off at the

31. Stegner, *Beyond the Hundredth Meridian*, 127–33.
32. Etulain and Stegner, *Conversations*, 181.
33. Stegner, *Beyond the Hundredth Meridian,* 354.
34. Stegner, *Beyond the Hundredth Meridian,* 227.
35. Stegner, *Beyond the Hundredth Meridian,* 315.
36. Stegner, *Beyond the Hundredth Meridian,* 316.

knees. When he told a Senate subcommittee in 1890 that "it would be almost a criminal act to go on as we are doing now, and allow thousands and hundreds of thousands of people to establish homes where they cannot maintain themselves," he stuck his head in the lions' mouths. The "Western Senators and Congressmen ... stomped his *Arid Region* proposals to death," Stegner wrote.[37]

Powell believed that, absent government intervention, the West's water resources would be squandered in beggar-thy-neighbor usage policies and by the laissez-faire assumptions of the powerful Congressmen. He proved to be right, and only the Dust Bowl calamities of the twentieth century would prompt the federal government to start building dams and planning irrigation districts along the lines Powell had suggested.

Stegner called Powell a "prophet," and his country chose to honor the grizzled explorer and bureaucratic warrior by naming the massive Lake Powell, accumulated behind the Glen Canyon Dam, after him in 1963. Powell was the first white man to seriously explore Glen Canyon and the complicated system of Colorado River tributaries upstream into Utah. Now it is mainly under water, with many of its scenic treasures sacrificed to the twin gods of power generation and mass recreation.

---

37. Stegner, *Beyond the Hundredth Meridian,* 283.

FIVE

The Mormons Again

"I've been corrupted. Mormons are getting too wholesome for me." —Wallace Stegner to his literary agents Brandt & Brandt, 1963

After finishing the Powell biography, Stegner re-visited the Mormons in two different books: *The Gathering of Zion: The Story of the Mormon Trail* (1964) and his novel *Recapitulation* (1979), in which the aged Bruce Mason, narrator of *The Big Rock Candy Mountain*, returns to Salt Lake City to revisit his past.

One can imagine Benny DeVoto, who died in 1955, hovering over the author's shoulder while Stegner wrote *Gathering*. Both men agreed that the mid-nineteenth century westward treks were the foundation stories of the American West. DeVoto's 1943 book, *The Year of Decision: 1846*, won the Pulitzer Prize. "It is a brave man who attempts to tell the story of the Mormon expulsion from Nauvoo after Bernard DeVoto's brilliant account in '*The Year of Decision: 1846*,'" Stegner wrote in the introduction to *Gathering*.[1] Later in life, he told an interviewer, "What I was trying to do in *The Gathering of Zion* was something very close to the Parkmanesque, Benny DeVoto thing—narrative history plus judgement."[2]

"My intention in *The Gathering of Zion* was clearly novelistic in its emphasis on human interest," Stegner explained, "but historical

1. Also from the introduction: "Having endured and *crossed to safety*, the Mormons began at once to transform their experience into myth." Emphasis added.

2. Richard W. Etulain and Wallace Stegner, *Conversations with Wallace Stegner on Western History and Literature*, revised edition (Salt Lake City: University of Utah Press, 1990), 117.

in that I wanted to be faithful to fact and record. *Because I was after visceral history.*"[3]

In his telling, Stegner's argument that "the Mormons were one of the principal forces in the settlement of the West"[4] was easy to prove:

> They were the most systematic, organized, disciplined and successful pioneers in our history; and their advantage over the random individualists who preceded them . . . came directly from their 'un-American' social and religious organization. Where Oregon emigrants and argonauts bound for the gold fields lost practically all their social cohesion en route, the Mormons moved like the Host of Israel they thought themselves. Far from loosening their social organization, the trail perfected it.[5]

Stegner loved the communitarian ethos, he loved the Mormons dancing around their campfires while sentinels kept watch for wolves and Indians, and he loved that the advance parties planted corn for settlers behind them. Stegner the litterateur, of course, savored the lucid trek journals, from William Clayton ("his old clerkly self, bitching secretly") to future church head Wilford Woodruff, who "will astonish us by reaching into his buggy and unlimbering his English fishing gear and becoming perhaps the first fly-fisherman in the history of the Rocky Mountains."[6] Stegner also served up a rare Gentile encomium for Joseph Smith: "Even an unbeliever is brought to the perception that the man who started all this was no mere charlatan, Peepstone Joe. This was a mighty imagination, a man with an extraordinary capacity to move men."[7]

Stegner was miffed that the Mormons' Church History Library refused to help him with the project. He thought their lack of cooperation divided the field into either "faith-sustaining" or "anti-Mormon" books. "The Mormons get defensive and the non-Mormons blow [the history of the church] up into something more than it is," he wrote, "and controversy and dull prose are magnified again. The only

---

3. Wallace Stegner, "On the Writing of History," in *The Sound of Mountain Water: The Changing American West* (New York: Vintage, 2017), 208. Emphasis added.

4. Wallace Stegner, *The Gathering of Zion: The Story of the Mormon Trail* (Lincoln, NB and London: University of Nebraska Press, 1981), 7.

5. Stegner, *Gathering*, 6.

6. Stegner, *Gathering,* 113 ff.

7. Stegner, *Gathering,* 312.

way to get away from attack-and-defense history, it seems to me, is to throw the archives open to everybody."[8]

At the end of *Gathering*, he summarized: "I write as a non-Mormon not a Mormon-hater. Except as it affected the actions of the people I write of, I do not deal with the Mormon faith: I do not believe it, but I do not quarrel with it either." In "A Word on Bibliography," he named four historians who "seem to me worthy of complete trust": DeVoto, Fawn Brodie, Dale Morgan, and Juanita Brooks. He must have realized that three of the four—DeVoto, Brodie, and Brooks—had crossed swords with Mormon officialdom, and more than once.

Dale Morgan and Stegner had a lively correspondence concerning *Gathering*. (Morgan addressed one letter to "Dear Elder Stegner.") After Stegner published a long article in *Holiday* magazine about Utah, he learned that feathers had been ruffled in Zion. Perhaps not surprisingly, as Stegner re-told one of his favorite tales about "the swearing Apostle," J. Golden Kimball. "J. Golden was President of the Council of Seventies," Stegner wrote, "but he sometimes backslid, took a drink, swore from the pulpit. The Church reprimanded him time after time, but actually let him get away with murder because he was the most effective orator, the kindliest man, and the best-loved official in the hierarchy. 'They can't throw me out,' J. Golden used to remark with a grin. 'I repent too damn fast.'"

"I am not surprised that the church is disturbed over the article in *Holiday*," Stegner wrote to Morgan. "It seems to me utterly impossible to write anything about the church except from within the hierarchy and avoid upsetting the first presidency."[9]

Stegner also cultivated friendships with Brodie, Brooks, and church historian Leonard Arrington. Among Stegner's papers is a 1973 Arrington letter proffering $1,000 for Stegner to comment on a draft biography of businessman David Eccles, a devout Mormon said to be Utah's first millionaire. (Eccles was also the subject of a famous 1915 lawsuit which declared a son by a plural wife to be a

8. Jackson Benson, *Wallace Stegner: His Life and Work* (New York: Viking Penguin, 1996), 287.

9. Box 18 fd. 53, Wallace Stegner Papers, J. Willard Marriott Library, University of Utah, Salt Lake City.

legitimate heir to his estate.[10]) Stegner took several months to write a fifteen-page critique of the book. "The critique was a wonderful manual on how to write a biography," Arrington recorded in his diary.[11]

More intriguingly, Stegner found a publisher for Brooks's Mountain Meadows Massacre manuscript. In his role as a West Coast scout for publisher Houghton Mifflin, Stegner sent the book to Boston headquarters. "Unfortunately, it strikes us as too much of a PhD thesis to be a trade publication," editor Austin Olney wrote to Stegner. Brooks told Stegner she was "not at all surprised … it was done with the idea of learning the facts and presenting them for the few who might be interested: students of Western history, L.D.S. who have never been quite satisfied with the accepted church story, and a few curious who have heard of the incident." But Stegner persevered. In August 1949, Stegner—by now a faculty member at Stanford—informed Brooks, "I was delighted to learn yesterday from Donald Bean that the Stanford Press is going to do your Mountain Meadows book. It's a book which eminently deserves publication and I admire your courage in bringing it out."[12]

In August 1963, Stegner confided to his literary agency that writing *Gathering* had tired him out, and "I've been corrupted. Mormons are getting too wholesome for me."[13] But the book was worth the effort. Jackson Benson called *Gathering* "a major contribution to the literature of the movement west … the story lives and breathes with such vividness that it would seem to have interest for any reader, whether the reader cares about the West and the Western Movement or not."[14]

Unbeknownst to Stegner, he had fans in Zion. Gordon B. Hinckley, church president from 1995 to 2008, told writer Harold Schindler that *The Gathering of Zion* was his favorite book. (Hinckley and Stegner were classmates at the University of Utah.) In 2000, Hinckley told *The Salt Lake Tribune*: "His little book on the

---

10. "Utah Court Upholds a Plural Marriage," *The New York Times*, July 17, 1915.

11. Leonard Arrington, *Confessions of a Mormon Historian*, vol. 1 (Salt Lake City: Signature Books, 2017), 862.

12. Box 43, fd. 47, Wallace Stegner Papers.

13. Benson, *Wallace Stegner*, 287–88.

14. Benson, *Wallace Stegner*, 298.

Mormons is a very moving book. He's done a good job, and I have enjoyed it. I've quoted on it, extensively at various times."[15]

The kind words would have come as no surprise. "No one is so popular among the Saints as a Gentile who expresses a good opinion of them," Stegner drily noted in *Gathering*.[16]

Recapitulation belongs to the tail end of Stegner's work, when he composed several successful novels with aging narrators either looking back on their lives (*Spectator Bird*, *Crossing to Safety*) or waxing embittered about modern life and the younger generation (*All the Little Live Things*). *Angle of Repose* also has an aging, infirm narrator at odds with the younger generation, but it aspires to tell a grander tale, a complicated, historical love story set during the taming of the West.

Recapitulation was not Stegner's first recapitulation. That would be *Wolf Willow: A History, a Story, and a Memory of the Last Plains Frontier*, which he published in 1962. Stegner and his wife bought a small mobile camper and lived in his childhood home of Eastend, Saskatchewan for three weeks while he researched the book. The couple traveled incognito, and whenever possible, declined to reveal their identity. With occasionally amusing results. The woman who furnished the electricity for their camper told Wallace and Mary that if they wanted to know more about the area, they should read *The Big Rock Candy Mountain*.[17]

Like many a visitor to childhood haunts, Stegner remembered everything as being bigger—the river, the swimming hole, the footbridge. He wrote a letter from Eastend to his friends Phil and Peg Gray, his neighbors in Vermont:

> Revisiting the childhood home ... [is] like an especially vivid but believed-in dream, has to be accepted as real, and that's an astonishing thing, almost as astonishing as the syntax of this sentence.

In *Recapitulation,* Bruce Mason, who scuttled off to law school at the end of *The Big Rock Candy Mountain*, is a high-level, globe-trotting diplomat who has been called back to Salt Lake City to settle his late aunt's estate. It is a nicely written, later-in-life retelling

15. Will Bagley, "'Except As a Friend': Wallace Stegner Among the Mormons," *Utah Historical Quarterly* 78, no. 2 (2010): 115.

16. Stegner, *Gathering*, 144.

17. Benson, *Wallace Stegner*, 206.

and reliving of the young Stegner's formative years. He describes his high school and college friends in recognizable detail. The fictional, tennis-playing Joe Mulder of both *Mountain* and *Recapitulation* was Stegner's close friend and teammate Jack Irvine, whose father, both in fiction and in real life, owned the rug and linoleum store where Stegner worked as a young man.

The Mulder/Irvines formed part of Stegner's support system when his own father and mother failed him. They were Mormons, but Stegner's favorite kind of Mormons—

> Jack Mormons, the Mulders did not tithe or go to meeting, but they kept the strenuous Mormon sense of stewardship. Having talents, one improved them. Having money or position, one tried to use it for the public good.[18]

The seasoned diplomat takes an evening walk to find the Mulders' house.

> Now after a long absence he stood before their house reminding himself that they really had treated him as a son, and that he owed them nearly everything—the job that J.J. gave him and innocently exploited him in, the independence the job had promoted, the affection they let him freely share. He supposed he was their faith in self-improvement made manifest, the object of a Mormon proselytizing impulse not lost but only redirected. He corroborated their belief that anyone could take hold of himself and make himself into something better, happier, richer. *It was an American, especially a Western, as well as a Mormon notion.*[19]

The girl whom the young Bruce Mason falls in love with, Nola, was Juanita Crawford, who died at age 69, nineteen years before Stegner. Crawford and Stegner were engaged, but she jilted him and married his close friend Francis Marvin Broberg, who clerked with Stegner at I. & M. Rug and Linoleum on State Street.[20] Crawford's nephew told

18. Stegner, *Recapitulation*, 109.

19. Stegner, *Recapitulation*, 109. Emphasis added.

20. In the novel, Bruce Mason has a brief fling with Nola's roommate, Holly, "a delighted little girl playing Life" who leaves Utah to find her fortune in Shanghai. Juanita Crawford's Salt Lake City roommate was Peg Foster, a journalist who interviewed Mao Tse-Tung in his mountain hideaway before the Communist revolution in China. When she died in 1997, the Chinese government honored her with a memorial service in the Great Hall of the People in Tiananmen Square.

Benson that his father called Stegner a "soda jerk," an epithet reserved for those who didn't take up the ranching life in Utah.[21]

The climactic scene of *Recapitulation* is Nola's sister's Mormon wedding in the mountains above Salt Lake City. These are Stegner's beloved, not-so-observant Mormons: Nola's brother Buck bums a cigarette from young Bruce, and in return offers a swig from a "partly emptied fifth of unlabeled red eye." And indeed, the father tries to talk to Bruce about "cattle, and alfalfa, and grazing permits and water rights."

The wedding convinces the stripling version of the mature diplomat that, despite his love for Salt Lake City, he can't make it his home. Surveying Nola's family, he views himself as

> An impostor, he knows that every single aspect of his background, if it were known, would be a black mark against him, and their solidarity makes him half envious. He feels how satisfying it would be to belong to some tribe or family, and though he feels superior to this one, he does not dismiss the notion of a not unfriendly alliance.[22]

At the very end of the book, having arranged his aunt's funeral, the unmarried Bruce Mason realizes that his family line will end with him. "He felt like the last survivor of a star-crossed family," Stegner wrote

> He felt like the puzzled son of a feckless father—boomer, dreamer, schemer, self-deceiver, bootlegger, eventually murderer and suicide, always burden, always enigma, always the harsh judge who must be appeased. He felt like the last remaining spectator at the last act of a play he had not understood.[23]

In the novel, Bruce Mason finally places a headstone on his father's grave. Stegner, his real-life counterpart, chose to leave his father's grave in Salt Lake Cemetery unmarked, as it remains today.

---

21. Benson, *Wallace Stegner*, 380.
22. Stegner, *Recapitulation*, 198.
23. Stegner, *Recapitulation*, 274.

SIX

Those Who Can, Teach

"He was like Vince Lombardi, and we were the Green Bay Packers of fiction writing."—Ken Kesey

Wallace Stegner was the proverbial man of parts. Historian, novelist, critic, and environmental activist, he was also one of the best-known writing teachers of the twentieth century. He earned that reputation during his twenty-five years as director of the Stanford Writing Program.

Stegner had taught writing before at Harvard, and perhaps most notably alongside Robert Frost and his friend DeVoto at the Bread Loaf Writers Conference, which met for the final two weeks of August every summer in Middlebury, Vermont. It was his Bread Loaf colleague Edith Mirrielees who recommended him for the Stanford job. Stanford landed a big fish. In 1946, Stegner was already the author of five novels, one an award winner—*Remembering Laughter*—and one a best seller—*The Big Rock Candy Mountain*—to say nothing of his well-received non-fiction book *Mormon Country*.

The Stanford program, renamed the Wallace Stegner Fellowship in 1973, has become the stuff of legend. The first crop of students was mainly older veterans parachuting (figuratively) into Stanford on the GI Bill. One was Eugene Burdick, a decorated Navy veteran who occasionally showed up in class wearing his uniform grays. Burdick was a shooting star; the story he showed to get into the program won an O. Henry Award, and he would go on to win a Rhodes Scholarship. Later, with William Lederer, another Navy veteran, he would co-author two huge best-sellers, *The Ugly American* and *Fail-Safe*.

Stegner looked back on those immediate post-war years of teaching as a halcyon period because he preferred teaching adult men and women, whose careers had been delayed by the war years, to teaching younger students. He savored the "mature, experienced, highly motivated men and women with hard experience, serious minds, and an urge to catch up lost time" who populated his first seminars.[1]

The second wave, who enrolled in the program during the late 1950s and 1960s would prove to be equally accomplished, and more contentious. "Taken collectively, the writing fellows of the new era were . . . far from [Stegner's] favorites, though he remained unfailingly gracious toward them," journalist Daniel Arnold wrote. "In style, compositional philosophy and persona, Stegner found himself on one tectonic plate while so many of his students sailed off on another."[2]

One young student embarking on his own idiosyncratic voyage was University of Oregon graduate Ken Kesey, who came to Stanford on a Woodrow Wilson fellowship in 1960. Kesey was an anomaly, a student intellectual who never completely abandoned his jock persona. He had wrestled at Oregon and almost qualified for the Olympics. A potent myth arose about the purported enmity between Stegner and the younger writer, a print-the-legend story that has elements of truth and falsehood. For instance, when Kesey made landfall in Palo Alto, Stegner wasn't even there. Kesey's first teachers at Stanford were Malcolm Cowley and Frank O'Connor; Stegner was away on sabbatical.

"The minute Ken Kesey walked into the Stegner Fellowship Class in Fiction, at Stanford in September of 1960, he made it plain that he meant to be the stud-duck—in today's parlance, the alpha male," was how classmate Larry McMurtry (who would later marry Kesey's widow) described his friend's arrival at Stanford. Kesey was a thicket of sharp elbows. McMurtry notes that by sitting next to the teacher, and by choosing to read his unpublished manuscript of *One Flew Over the Cuckoo's Nest* ahead of the several published novelists in the class caused the other students to "bristle." McMurtry himself

1. Jackson Benson, *Wallace Stegner: His Life and Work* (New York: Viking Penguin, 1996), 164.

2. Daniel Arnold, "Westword, Bound," *Stanford Magazine*, July 2021.

had just sold his first novel, *Horseman, Pass By*, which would be made into the movie *Hud*.

"Then [we] relaxed and decided to be bemused, rather than annoyed," McMurtry wrote. "Why? Because Ken Kesey was a very winning man, and he won us."[3]

In the course of his lifetime, Kesey said many silly things about Stegner, to what end it is hard to imagine. For instance, he once wrote that "Stegner had traveled across the Great Plains and reached the Pacific. . . . That was, as far as he was concerned, the edge of the continent, and he thought you were supposed to stop there." But Kesey purportedly wanted to go further, to cross into new synaptic frontiers:

> As soon as I took LSD, and he drank Jack Daniel's [sic], we drew the line between us right there. . . . Ever since then, I have felt kind of impelled into the future by Wally, by his dislike of what I was doing, what we were doing. That was the kiss of approval in some way.[4]

Kesey wasn't bedeviled by consistency when it came to describing Stegner. "When I asked him once if Stegner had been a good teacher," Oregon novelist John Daniel wrote, "he replied, 'He was better than a teacher. He was like Vince Lombardi, and we were the Green Bay Packers of fiction writing.' Kesey gave that same answer, publicly, many times."[5]

But on other occasions, Kesey went out of his way to be hurtful. He accused Stegner of "writing to a class-room and to his colleagues" instead of honestly—a barb honed to wound the prideful Stegner. Kesey baited Stegner unnecessarily. For instance, when asked what he learned from Stegner, he replied, "Just never to teach in college."[6] Kesey himself did end up teaching for a year at the University of Oregon.[7] The novelist John Daniel remembered, "When I asked on the phone why it was [he and Stegner] hadn't gotten along, Kesey replied: 'Because I was a better writer than him.'"[8]

3. Larry McMurtry, "On the Road," *New York Review of Books*, Dec. 5, 2002.
4. Benson, *Wallace Stegner*, 253.
5. Arnold, "Westword, Bound."
6. Benson, *Wallace Stegner*, 250.
7. John Daniel, "The Prankster-in-Chief Moves On," *Open Spaces*, Dec. 2001.
8. Daniel, "Prankster."

Maybe, and maybe not.

The gentlemanly Stegner generally retreated to higher ground when commenting on Kesey: "I think they all make more of my antagonism to Kesey than there was there. Personally, I was never sympathetic to any of his ideas because I thought many of his ideas were half baked.... [But] we got along in class perfectly well. I liked his writing most of the time very well."[9]

Robert Stone, who would later become a much-decorated novelist, was a fan of Kesey's who got along with both men. He told Daniel Arnold that "Stegner saw Kesey and what he represented as a threat to civilization and intellectualism and sobriety. And Ken was a threat to all those values." "But ... Ken was so exciting, and just plain fun, that we were not about to line up against each other on ideological grounds."[10]

The Kesey-Stegner saga makes for lively reading. But who would expect these two very different talents, and men from different generations, to get along? And why should they? In 1961, when they first met, Stegner was fifty-two years old and Kesey was twenty-five. Kesey claimed that he conjured up the famous protagonist of *Cuckoo's Nest*, Chief Bromden, in a peyote-induced vision, hardly the kind of inspiration Wallace Stegner would boast of.

As a footnote, it's hard not to see how positively Stegnerian some of Kesey's prose sounds. In a lengthy appreciation of his friend, McMurtry quoted a lyric passage from Kesey's second novel, *Sometimes a Great Notion*, that sounds very close in tone to passages of *Wolf Willow*, Stegner's Saskatchewan memoir. Describing the Wakonda Agua River on the western slopes of the Oregon Coastal Range, Kesey wrote:

> Then, through bearberry and salmonberry, blueberry and blackberry, the branches crashing into creeks, into streams. Finally, in the foothills, through tamarack and sugar pine, shittim bark and silver spruce—and the green and blue mosaic of Douglas fir—the actual river falls five hundred feet ... and look: opens out upon the fields.

How did Stegner teach? By most accounts, quite well. "Wally

9. Benson, *Wallace Stegner*, 249.
10. Benson, *Wallace Stegner*, 253.

was very businesslike," his student Al Young said. "He would tell you exactly what he thought, and he would be considerate of your feelings, but he would not pull punches. He had a manner, a style, that was gentle. And he would give you bad news in a gentle way."[11]

Wendell Berry, a student who would later become a good friend of Stegner's, said "his performance was really like a good foreman.... He gave you good technical criticism and good technical criticism comes from somewhere. I think you always know that. He would get down to the nuts and bolts of it."[12]

Interviewed in 2017, *Presumed Innocent* author Scott Turow remarked:

> Wally emphasized that writing a novel was, first and foremost, a job, which, like any other job, required you to work every day. Wally himself wrote two pages each day of the year except Christmas, but for those less dogged, he insisted that at least 30 minutes a day was required.[13]

On occasion, Stegner would invert the teacher-student dynamic and bring his own fiction to be critiqued by the workshop. Ed McLanahan remembered when Stegner brought in some pages from his Palo Alto novel, *All the Little Live Things*, which would be published in 1967. "Everybody was really knocked out by it," McLanahan said, one student going so far as to call it "obviously a Pulitzer Prize-winning book."[14]

In his relatively rare public comments about teaching fiction, Stegner perhaps predictably leaned on some old verities. In a brief essay called "A Note on Technique," he included a "few rules of thumb" about writing:

> 1. Start in the middle of things, begin in motion. 2. Stay in motion by not letting the summary intrude.... 3. Never explain too much; a reader is offended if he cannot participate and use his mind and imagination, and a story loses much of its suspense the moment everything is explained. 4. Stay out of your story.... 5. Don't show off in your style....

11. Benson, *Wallace Stegner*, 259.
12. Benson, *Wallace Stegner*, 262.
13. "The Book Report," *The Toronto Globe and Mail*, May 26, 2017.
14. Benson, *Wallace Stegner*, 266.

7. Stopping a story is as hard as saying goodnight. Learn to do it cleanly, without leftovers or repetitions.[15]

Stegner was considerably older than his charges and he had generally conservative tastes in fiction. "I don't really aspire to write a novel which can be read backwards as well as forward . . . which, in effect, tries to create a novel by throwing all the pieces in the bag and shaking the bag," he told an interviewer in 1982.[16] That same year, Stegner wrote a short, funny essay, "Goodbye to All T—t," in which he allowed that while any and all vocabulary was welcome in the writing seminar, he himself was never quick to use profanity in his fiction. "Some acts, like some words, were never meant to be casual. That is why houses contain bedrooms and bathrooms. ... So I am not going to say shit before any more ladies. I am going to hunt words that have not lost their sting, and it may be I shall have to go back to gentility to find them."[17]

Stegner could of course be relied on to generate the recommendations and publishing world contacts that were the mother's milk of literary academe. And he could display extraordinary acts of generosity towards his students. McLanahan told Benson that when Robert Stone developed a serious medical problem that generated significant bills at the university hospital, Stegner extended Stone's fellowship to preserve his medical insurance, and to allow him to keep the $1250 quarterly cash stipend. "And Mr. Stegner didn't even ask him to do so much as come to the class after he got back on his feet, which everybody else was automatically expected to do."[18] [19]

Nothing lasts forever, and neither did Stegner's tenure at the writing program. It was certainly a plum assignment. Stanford had

15. Wallace Stegner, "A Note on Technique," in *On Teaching and Writing Fiction* (New York: Penguin, 2002), 94–95.

16. James R. Hepworth, *Stealing Glances: Three Interviews with Wallace Stegner* (Albuquerque, NM: University of New Mexico Press, 1980), 58.

17. Wallace Stegner, "Goodbye to All T—t," in *On Teaching and Writing Fiction,* Lynn Stegner, ed. (New York: Penguin, 2002), 81.

18. Benson, *Wallace Stegner,* 265.

19. The facts seem to align with McLanahan's account, but Stegner, speaking to interviewer James Hepworth, thought Stone was "quite wacky, really" and expressed skepticism about the brain affliction. "He got the notion in the middle of the year that he had a brain tumor. . . . He swore later they bored a hole into his head and blew him out with a pressure hose, but they didn't find any brain tumor."

hired him as a full professor with only a half-time teaching load, which left him ample opportunity to continue his book-writing career. Between 1946 and 1971, when he quit the Stanford job, he published six novels and six significant works of non-fiction.

According to Benson, Stegner became enmeshed in English department politics during the 1960s and he didn't always emerge the winner. Avant-garde writers, such as postmodernist John Hawkes, started showing up on campus, courting his disapproval, as did Irving Howe, a pillar of the New York Jewish intelligentsia who was appointed a professor of American literature. Stegner correctly surmised that Howe wouldn't last long west of the Hudson River, and he didn't. Stegner and Mary feted Howe at the obligatory departmental cocktail parties, only to see him stalk out in disgust. Stegner called Howe "the rudest guy I've ever known." "He'd be invited to a cocktail party, and he'd sort of look around and decide there was no one to talk to ... and then he'd walk out."[20]

Howe quickly repatriated to New York, grumbling about "the dead West." In his autobiography, he wrote, "Something about California, a softening of the mind, makes it finally a second-rate culture, self-satisfied and self-adoring."

But it was a different kind of politics that prompted Stegner to resign peremptorily at the age of sixty-two. Stanford, like many university campuses, was awash in student protests, mainly against the Vietnam War, which Stegner and many other faculty members opposed. But the protests had an element of disrespect that Stegner found particularly noisome. When he returned from a sabbatical in 1968, his friend and colleague Richard Scowcroft informed him that the graduate students "didn't want to sit around the table. They didn't even want chairs. They wanted me to move the furniture out so they could just stretch out on the floor."

Stegner "was not exactly a conservative," essayist Bill Croke has observed, "but rather an old-fashioned—now out-of-fashion—sort of liberal."[21] The venerable teacher believed in decorum and mutual respect, ideals that he saw inexplicably challenged on the progressive

---

20. Benson, *Wallace Stegner*, 340.

21. Bill Croke, "WANTED: The West of Wallace Stegner," *Washington Examiner*, Apr. 19, 1999.

campus. He gritted his teeth, but only for a short while. In 1971, he noticed an article in the student newspaper that attacked him personally. His officemate Wilfred Stone reported Stegner saying "That ends it. I'm not going to do anything more. I'm washing my hands of this whole business." "And he was done with it," Stone wrote, "he was sort of done with the [whole] modern generation."[22]

The Stegner Fellowship lived on—it lives on to this day—but without Wallace Stegner.

In 1990, Wendell Berry, the farmer/writer who turned out to be Stegner's favorite student, read a letter written by Stegner at former student Edward Abbey's funeral in the Utah desert. In the letter, Stegner called Abbey "a red-hot moment in the conscience of the country." Three years later, Berry wrote a letter extolling the deceased Stegner, calling him "not a red-hot moment, but one that was luminous, clarifying, and steady."

Speaking to Benson, Berry elaborated on his affection for his former teacher:

> I don't think he was the kind of teacher who tried to make his students into followers, but the outcome of my acquaintance with him is that I've become his follower in lots of ways. And it didn't happen at Stanford, but when I came away, when I came back and settled here [in Kentucky] and began to read his non-fiction books—*Wolf Willow*, *Beyond the Hundredth Meridian*, the DeVoto biography, and the conservation essays.... I think he's probably the first American fiction writer to be a conservationist.[23]

22. Benson, *Wallace Stegner*, 341 ff.
23. Benson, *Wallace Stegner*, 263.

SEVEN

Stegner in the World

"We simply need that wild country available to us. . . .
For it can be a means of reassuring ourselves of our sanity
as creatures, as part of the geography of hope."
—Wallace Stegner, "Essay on Wilderness"

It "was all Benny's doing," is how Stegner remembered his initial foray into environmental activism. That is true. From his perch as "The Easy Chair" columnist for *Harper's*, DeVoto had started speaking out against the Eisenhower Administration's too-casual, too-free-market attitude toward the national parks and federal lands. In the early 1950s, DeVoto was the proverbial voice crying in the desert.

When Stegner wrote to DeVoto expressing outrage over the efforts by some members of Congress to privatize federal lands, De Voto urged his friend to "get into print" with his feelings. And he did. "Benny DeVoto has commanded me to write an article on what is likely to happen to the conservation program in the West under the Republicans," Stegner wrote to one of his literary agents in 1953. "My last chapter on Powell leads me into the conservation business anyway so I might as well try to gratify Benny and turn a penny all at the same time."[1]

Stegner published an article in *The Reporter* in May 1953 outlining his fears that Eisenhower & Co. might give free rein to the "powerful and persistent private interests that for years have tried to

1. Philip Fradkin, *Wallace Stegner and the American West* (Berkeley, CA: University of California Press, 2009), 184.

corral the West's land, water, timber and water power."[2] In the process, Stegner introduced his readers to John Wesley Powell, whom he heralded as America's first conservationist: "Conservation began, actually, with Powell's Report on the Lands of the Arid Region in 1878. It hardly had time to raise its head before it was stamped to death by enraged Western Congressmen."

Stegner repeated his full-throated endorsement of Powell, the man who once explained to Montanans that "all the great values of this territory have ultimately to be measured to you in acre feet." Powell, per Stegner, was "talking at least sixty years too soon. They called him a revolutionary and they stopped him cold for ten years."

David Brower, the newly appointed executive director of the Sierra Club, saw Stegner's article and approached him to edit and contribute to a book on Dinosaur National Monument, a wilderness park in Utah, which was threatened by a proposed dam. Brower wanted the book to be the first in a series that would thrust the Club directly into policy disputes, trading its previously sedate profile as a membership organization for outdoorsy types for a more combative policy role. He correctly thought Stegner would respond to saving the Monument, which was first explored (of course) by Powell.

Published in 1954 by Alfred A. Knopf—with an essay by the famous editor himself, who did not take kindly to being edited by Stegner—the book sold well and was distributed to every member of Congress. In his anchor essay, Stegner showcased some of the lapidary prose for which he quickly became famous, offering up a vision of an environment improved by conservation:

> It is a better world with some buffalo left in it, a richer world with some gorgeous canyons unmarred by signboards, hot dog stands … or high-tension lines, undrowned by power or irrigation reservoirs.

It is not "only the buffalo and the trumpeter swan who needs sanctuaries," Stegner concluded. "Our own species is going to need them too."[3]

The book proved to be part of a successful lobbying campaign. The dam was never built, and the Dinosaur Monument was saved.

---

2. Wallace Stegner, "One-Fourth of a Nation: Public Lands and Itching Fingers," *The Reporter*, Dec. 5, 1953.

3. Wallace Stegner, ed., *This Is Dinosaur* (New York: Alfred A. Knopf, 1955).

But in the political horse-trading among the Bureau of Reclamation, the Army Corps of Engineers, and Western politicians, the Sierra Club decided not to oppose construction of the equally controversial Glen Canyon Dam on the Colorado River. "Having saved Dinosaur, we accepted the ruin of Glen Canyon, which was not very smart of us," Stegner commented.[4] Brower later admitted that Stegner had told him that the scenery above Glen Canyon was more worthy of preservation than Dinosaur. "Wallace Stegner had told me, 'Strictly between us, doesn't hold a candle to Glen.' I have worn sackcloth and ashes ever since, convinced that I could have saved the place if I had simply got off my duff."[5]

In 1969, Stegner published a poignant essay, "Glen Canyon Submersus," describing his March 1965 boat trip on Lake Powell, which stretched for 150 miles behind the dam. He meditated on the many wonders submerged beneath him; for instance, the Music Temple, a grotto with towering, painted walls, was underwater. He wrote, "Another fifty feet of water would submerge the Gregory Natural Bridge and flood the floor of the Cathedral of the Desert." Nature would eventually play many tricks. The Cathedral and the Natural Bridge were eventually flooded but have now come back into view due to years of drought.

The "Submersus" essay displays Stegner's instinct for compromise. "Though they have diminished it, they haven't utterly ruined it," he wrote of the lost Glen Canyon marvels. The panoramic views are better, of course, because you can see more of the surrounding countryside riding on 340 feet of water: "Navajo Canyon is splendid despite the flooding of its green bottom that used to provide pasture for the stolen horses of raiders. Forbidden Canyon that leads to Rainbow Bridge is lessened, but still marvelous; it is like going by boat to Petra."

> Worst of all are the places I remember that are now irretrievably gone. Surging up-lake on my second day, I look over my shoulder and recognize the swamped and hidden entrance to Hidden Passage Canyon, on whose bar we camped eighteen years ago.... Once that canyon was

4. Richard W. Etulain and Wallace Stegner, *Conversations with Wallace Stegner on Western History and Literature*, revised edition (Salt Lake City: University of Utah Press, 1990), 169.

5. David Brower, "Let the River Run Through It," *Sierra Magazine*, March/April 1997.

> a pure delight to walk in; now it is only another slot with water in it, a thing to poke a motorboat into for five minutes and then roar out again.[6]

"It strikes me, even in my exhilaration, with the consciousness of loss. In gaining the lovely and the usable, we have given up the incomparable," he concluded.

But those thoughts came later. Stegner's first interaction with Brower led to a long relationship with the Sierra Club, including a three-year stint on its board, from 1964 to 1966. That placed him at the center of a furious dispute between his friends: Brower and the legendary photographer Ansel Adams, among others. Brower wanted to radicalize the Club, and the Club's older supporters, like Stegner and Adams, resisted. "Fuck the Sierra Club" bumper stickers popping up on California highways discomfited Stegner, as did Brower's increasingly messianic commitment to environmental issues.

The two parted company, dramatically, when Brower told Mary Stegner that Wally should stop writing novels and pay attention to the fate of the planet. Then Stegner spotted a wire service story in which Brower pitted Club "progressives" against "traditionalists." As Stegner read it, he and Adams were being derided as fuddy-duddies "who want to keep the club's old image as a hiking organization." He unleashed a salvo in his local newspaper, *The Palo Alto Times*, averring that "Brower has ceased to be what he was. He has been bitten by some worm of power." The upshot was that the board lost confidence in Brower, who left the Sierra Club to found a new organization, The Friends of the Earth.[7]

None of this sat well with Stegner, who abhorred confrontation. He confessed to interviewer James Hepworth that "I am not a good soldier in the environmental armies because I don't seem to work well in bodies with other people." He found it hard to summon the requisite zealotry for the cause, which was why he rarely addressed it in his fiction, to avoid sounding "doctrinaire."[8]

---

6. There is now less water in Lake Powell than when Stegner took his boat ride in 1965. In October, 2024, Powell was 123 feet below "full pool," making it about ten feet lower than when Stegner visited, while it was still filling up.

7. Jackson Benson, *Wallace Stegner: His Life and Work* (New York: Viking Penguin, 1996), 325–35.

8. James Hepworth, *Stealing Glances: Three Interviews with Wallace Stegner* (Albuquerque, NM: University of New Mexico Press, 1998), 109.

The Sierra Club represented only one facet of his environmental work. When John F. Kennedy took office in 1961, Stegner sent a copy of his John Wesley Powell biography to Stewart Udall, the new Secretary of the Interior. Udall had served as a Congressman from Arizona. "Precisely the kind of Secretary we wanted," Stegner said, "a Westerner with an intimate knowledge of the dry country but with a distaste for the economics of liquidation that was killing it." Udall had a poetic sensibility that Stegner admired. As Secretary, he floated the idea of designating the birthplaces of Carl Sandburg and Robert Frost as "national poetic monuments," a notion that never panned out.[9] [10]

Udall recruited Stegner as a special assistant and "artist in residence" at the Department of the Interior, an appointment that lasted for just four months. Stegner's main contribution may have been to encourage Udall to write his book *The Quiet Crisis*, a popular history of environmentalists such as Henry David Thoreau, Frederick Law Olmsted, and John Muir. Published in 1963 with a foreword by President Kennedy, the book became a bestseller.[11] Stegner then served on the National Parks Advisory Board, which he eventually left because his travel schedule prevented him from attending meetings.

Embedded inside Interior, Stegner saw real decisions being made. He remembered advocating strenuously against two proposed Grand Canyon dams. But he realized that that corner of the Southwest was going to get electric power by hook or by crook; not only did Udall have an Arizona constituency, but his brother Morris now occupied his former Congressional seat. "Eventually we all agreed ... that these power dams be supplanted by coal-fired plants," he told an

9. Wallace Stegner, "The Artist as Environmental Advocate," an oral history conducted in 1982 by Ann Lage, Sierra Club History Series, Regional Oral History Office, The Bancroft Library, University of California, Berkeley, https://digitalassets.lib.berkeley.edu/roho/ucb/text/stegner_wallace.pdf, p. 22.

10. Stegner thought Udall possessed an inbred "stewardship" of Western lands. "Being a Mormon, he had some notion of it, because Mormons did have some notion of it. They were an agricultural people ... his family in Arizona, I'm sure, had a respect for land because they had to work for it and with it to make it pay" [*Sierra Club History Series*, 1982].

11. Benson, *Wallace Stegner*, 279.

interviewer. "So now we've got the coal plant at Four Corners and in Page. Now [laughs] this is not good."[12]

Stegner recalled one memorable incident from his board service: While it had become customary to designate presidential birthplaces as national historic sites, the designation always took place posthumously. So, when the White House "suggested" that President Lyndon Johnson's birthplace become a site, Stegner and his advisory board colleagues all voted no. "Then we got word from Stewart that we damn well had to [laughter]," he explained. "So swallow and hold your nose and do it."[13]

How does the saying go? Think globally, act locally? On May 25, 1962, Stegner issued a public invitation to a "Skyline picnic" "in the newly annexed part of Palo Alto." (Stegner lived in Los Altos Hills, just south of Palo Alto.) "This is a picnic with a purpose," Stegner wrote, and the purpose was to create a grassroots organization to monitor development in the gorgeous hills west of Stanford and Palo Alto, a group to be named The Committee for Green Foothills. The local residents had just lost a battle to keep "factories out of the foothills" when Stanford University erected its massive Industrial Park, "raising concerns that all of the foothills would disappear if a more concerted effort was not made to save them," according to the organization's website.

In a 1982 interview for the Sierra Club History Series, Stegner recalled many battles—most of them with ever-expanding Stanford—over the years. "You win some and lose some," he said, "and you win far fewer than you lose." One win was preventing Palo Alto from building skyscrapers up to its skyline; instead, the area became open space. "So now of course Palo Alto has all these foothill lands, and they're holding them effectively as a land bank. Thank God."

His chosen hometown of Los Altos Hills next door, he said, was not so fortunate: It "has been developed in a way that would make a cannibal cry."

The organization Stegner co-founded has since changed its name to Green Foothills and has broadened its purview to protect open space and natural resources in counties beyond Palo Alto. Supporters

12. Stegner, "Environmental Advocate," 15.
13. Stegner, "Environmental Advocate," 19.

who give over $500 annually join the Stegner Giving Circle, named for Green Foothills' best-known founder.[14]

As he grew older, Stegner developed mixed feelings about the environmental movement, and vice versa. In his 1974 biography of DeVoto, he wrote waspishly that what had been known as "conservation advocacy" had "developed into something like a religion of Nature, shared by hippies, housewives, mountain climbers, river runners, fishermen and many other kinds of Americans."[15] His occasionally crotchety 1967 novel, *All the Little Live Things*, simultaneously complains about development in the Peninsula hills where he lived and portrays a back-to-the-earth squatter as a menace to society—and worse.

To the new generation of environmentalists, Stegner looked a little long in the tooth. In 1969, Edward Abbey took a swipe at his former teacher in a *New York Times* review of Stegner's essay collection, *The Sound of Mountain Water*. "His voice is that of a gentle and human liberalism," Abbey wrote, clearly not intending to compliment Stegner, "which believes that even the life of quiet desperation is still worth living. His fault is an excess of moderation, an extremity of forbearance." Citing Stegner's conflicted feelings about the Glen Canyon dam, Abbey asked why Stegner didn't call for its demolition, rather than accept its environmental depredations as a *fait accompli*.[16]

Abbey, nineteen years Stegner's junior, was cut from different cloth. His 1975 novel, *The Money Wrench Gang*, introduced the idea of eco-sabotage to a wide audience, and is often credited as the inspiration behind Earth First!, best known for tree-spikings to thwart logging companies, and other acts of eco-vandalism. In an interview a decade later, Stegner described Abbey as "an advocate in the Dave Brower pattern, even worse. Worse in the sense of more intransigent.... But a very lively writer. He's got a lot of readers. Has done a lot of good."[17] [18]

14. "About," Green Foothills, accessed Sep. 14, 2024, https://www.greenfoothills.org/about/.

15. Wallace Stegner, *The Uneasy Chair: A Biography of Bernard DeVoto* (New York: Doubleday, 1974), 321.

16. Edward Abbey, "The Sound of Mountain Water," *The New York Times,* June 8, 1969.

17. Stegner, "Environmental Advocate," 36.

18. Eight years later, Abbey extended an olive branch to his former teacher in the form of a postcard extolling *Angle of Repose*: "A splendid novel," Abbey wrote, "you had me in tears for nearly 400 pages" [Fradkin, *Wallace Stegner*, 130].

The collection that Abbey reviewed also contained Stegner's famous 1960 "Wilderness Letter," written in a few hours and submitted as part of an official filing by the Outdoor Recreation Resources Review Commission in support of the Wilderness Bill pending in Congress. The letter entered environmental history on the strength of Stegner's elegant characterization of wilderness areas as "the geography of hope." That slogan was reproduced on numerous wildlife posters, and it also became the title of a Sierra Club book of photographs by Eliot Porter.

In the text, Stegner asserted, forcefully, that "the wilderness *idea*" is an unrecognized "intangible and spiritual resource" that doesn't even have to be experienced to contribute to the common good. "The reminder and the reassurance that [wilderness] is still there is good for our spiritual health even if we never once in ten years set foot in it," he wrote.

He described himself as a child of the Canadian wilderness:

> On our Saskatchewan prairie, the nearest neighbor was four miles away, and at night we saw only two lights on all the dark roundling earth. The earth was full of animals—field mice, ground squirrels, weasels, ferrets, badgers, coyotes, burrowing owls, snakes. I knew them as my little brothers, fellow creatures, and I have never been able to look on animals in any other way since.... I hope I learned something from knowing intimately the creatures of the earth; I hope I learned something from looking a long way, from looking up, from being much alone.

He declined to mention his schoolboy awards for gopher genocide, waged with .22 rifles, traps, and "buckets of sweet-smelling strychnine-soaked wheat."[19]

"We simply need that wild country available to us," he concluded, "even if we never do more than drive to its edge and look in. For it can be a means of reassuring ourselves of our sanity as creatures, as part of the geography of hope."

The letter found an audience. Stewart Udall scrapped a prepared speech at a wilderness conference in San Francisco and read the Stegner letter instead. The *Washington Post* reproduced the text.

19. Wallace Stegner, *Wolf Willow: A History, a Story, and a Memory of the Last Plains Frontier* (New York: Penguin Classics, 2000), 275.

"Altogether, this letter, the labor of an afternoon," Stegner wrote, had "gone farther around the world than other writings on which I have spent years."[20]

20. Wallace Stegner, "Saga of a Letter: The Geography of Hope," *Living Wilderness*, December 1980, 43.

EIGHT

Tangle of Repose

"Stegner stole everything."
—Mary Ellen Williams Walsh on *Angle of Repose*

Wallace Stegner's long and well-lived life had many high watermarks, an image that, as a connoisseur of canyons, dams, and flash floods, he would have savored. One such moment would be the 1971 publication of *Angle of Repose*, his epic novel about a couple's tribulations against the backdrop of mining and hydrological projects in the West, which won the Pulitzer Prize for Fiction in 1972.

It is arguably the most Stegnerian of his books. It is long, like *The Big Rock Candy Mountain*, and it uses memory and recollection as a narrative device, as do *Recapitulation*, *Wolf Willow*, and *The Spectator Bird*. The protagonists of *Repose*, Susan and Oliver Ward, are mostly seeking their fortune in Stegner Country, the Great Basin between the Rockies and the Sierra.

The eloquent and enigmatic title refers to the steepest angle at which material can be piled up before it collapses. Throughout the book, the Wards seem to be teetering on the brink of collapse, in a suspended state of tense repose. Stegner allows himself a small joke at his own expense; when the elderly narrator's caretaker learns his idea for a title, she comments: "Is that a very good title? Will it sell? It sounds kind of . . . inert."

Repose brought Stegner a modicum of additional fame, some bitter frustration, and, eventually, vitriolic, posthumous condemnation of a kind he could never have understood. The novel should have been the capstone of his career. Instead, it became a recurring nuisance—on critical, personal, and ethical levels—that has dogged him into the present time.

I have heard schoolteachers marvel that the only thing some of their students seem to know about George Washington is, "Oh, he's the guy who owned slaves." When Stegner's name comes up in conversation these days, it's not unusual to hear, "Oh, he's the guy who plagiarized the famous novel, right?" No, but he's the guy who integrated huge swatches of another writer's unpublished writing into his masterwork and came to regret it.

Stegner's publisher, Doubleday, thought *Repose* would sell well, and budgeted a whopping $40,000 (about $300,000 in today's dollars) for advertising. The Book of the Month Club offered Stegner $125,000 for distribution rights (over $900,000 today), which, regrettably, his agent had already sold to the (Doubleday-owned) Literary Guild for less than half that sum.

As expected, the novel sold quickly out of the gate. Doubleday and Stegner had pinned their national sales hopes on coverage in *The New York Times*, which published both daily book reviews and the semi-authoritative *Sunday New York Times Book Review*. But the *Times* ignored *Repose* for two months, and when the newspaper first mentioned it, their columnist professed confusion over the book's twentieth-to-nineteenth-century flashback structure. "It is the work of a forthright craftsman," William DuBois wrote, with the caveat that "I reached page 569 convinced that an essential element was missing . . . the addict [of the well-made novel] can be forgiven for wanting something even better."

DuBois awarded Stegner an A minus grade. Praise of a kind, but not a coveted "selling" review.[1]

Out of the blue, about a year after publication, a unanimous jury awarded *Repose* the 1972 Pulitzer Prize, a gold-plated endorsement. Stegner was overjoyed, as he explained to his close friend Phil Gray:

> One of the nicest things about the Pulitzer Prize is all sorts of people call up, and wire, and write. It's bettern [sic] Christmas cards. . . . When a TV man asked how I felt, I said I felt humble, and Mary briskly kicked my shins. But I wasn't talking about the damn prize. Hell, I've deserved

1. William DuBois, "The Last Word: The Well-Made Novel," *The New York Times*, Aug. 9, 1971.

> that since my first book. . . . But I felt humble about that telephone ringing from all over, and really jubilant voices, as pleased for us as if it had happened to them.[2]

Just two weeks after the award, John Leonard, the editor of the *Times*'s *Book Review*, leapt into print to condemn the "long, apparently endless line of Pulitzer disappointments," exemplified, he wrote, by *Angle of Repose*. Because the fiction prize hadn't been awarded the previous year, Leonard expressed incredulity that "Mr. Stegner's novel is the only 'distinguished work of fiction by an American author' *in the last two years*." He went on to anathematize the Pulitzer jurors who settled for "whatever is comfortable, tame, toothless and affectionate—a pet instead of a work of art." In a parting salvo, he added: "We have obviously settled for pacifiers, and one hopes we choke on them."[3]

The arrow hit home. For the next two decades Stegner perceived himself, with no small ration of self-pity, as a writer shunned as a rube by the New York intelligentsia. A subsequent *New York Times* magazine cover story would misidentify him as "William Stegner," the "dean" of contemporary Western writers. Too Western, too old, too heterosexual, too white—the litany of complaints accumulated over the years, as we shall see.

Angle of Repose sold well after the Pulitzer boost and has never been out of print. It would lead a picaresque existence, starting just one year after the award, with its unlikely selection as a bicentennial-themed opera.

In 1973, Stegner's literary agency, Brandt & Brandt, received an inquiry from San Francisco mayor Joseph Alioto, who wanted to produce *Angle of Repose* for the San Francisco Opera, as part of the city's 1976 Bicentennial festivities. Carol Brandt promptly advised Stegner: "I take a dim view of having ANGLE OF REPOSE involved with the San Francisco Opera Co. You are quite right in saying that you don't want to do the libretto." One of her major concerns was that the sale of opera rights might jeopardize potential interest from

2. Philip Fradkin, *Wallace Stegner and the American West* (New York: Alfred A. Knopf, 2008), 249.

3. John Leonard, "The Pulitzer Prizes: Fail-Safe Again," *The New York Times*, May 14, 1972.

Hollywood. She had heard talk of possible TV mini-series adaptations of both *Repose* and *Big Rock Candy Mountain.*[4]

Those projects never went anywhere, but the opera ground forward. Oakley Hall, a California native and a veteran writer of Western fiction, was selected to write the libretto. Andrew Imbrie, a music professor at the University of California Berkeley, composed the score. Conductor John Mauceri, who had collaborated on the West Coast premiere of Benjamin Britten's *Death in Venice* in San Francisco, led the orchestra. He now remembers *Repose* as "a wonderful work; it was an enormous job, enormously difficult. I saw its beauty and I saw its complexity."[5]

According to Mauceri, *Repose* "was considered to be a huge success, it was the rare opera that got unanimously favorable reviews." In *The San Francisco Chronicle*, critic Robert Commanday called the performance an "absorbing, outstanding experience." *The San Francisco Examiner*'s critic, Alexander Fried, praised the work as "rare among new American opera." "Without a doubt, Imbrie's first major opera is an admirable accomplishment," Fried wrote. "Visually the entire 'Angle' was a tour de force of nervy ambition, charm and technical skills."[6]

Even though members of the International Association of Opera Directors, in San Francisco for their annual meeting, were in the audience, the opera was never performed after its brief, bicentennial run of five performances. But it inadvertently contributed to the smoldering, below-the-radar controversy that had been gathering momentum since the book's appearance.

To understand the *Repose* imbroglio, it helps to know what the novel is about. Retired historian Lyman Ward is researching and retelling the extraordinary life story of his grandmother Susan Burling Ward and her husband, a mining engineer assigned to extraction and irrigation projects in California, Colorado, and Mexico. Susan Ward is a fictional recreation of the talented writer and artist Mary

4. Box 27, fd. 13, Wallace Stegner Papers, J. Willard Marriott Library, University of Utah, Salt Lake City.

5. Mauceri, whose musical taste has become more conservative over the years, remembers Imbrie's score as "mostly atonal and twelve-tone." At the opening night party at Imbrie's house, Mauceri recalls, the Berkeley professor blasted Glenn Miller tunes from his stereo. "'Why didn't you write like that?' I asked him," Mauceri says. Imbrie's reply: "They'd never let me do that."

6. "Imbrie's 'Angle' Has Debut on Coast," *The New York Times*, Nov. 9, 1976.

Hallock Foote, whose work was coming to light just as Stegner committed to writing *Repose*.

Stegner was familiar with Mary Foote's rich and evocative letters and diaries, and even tried to convince a colleague to write her biography. He had also suggested to Foote's granddaughter, Janet Micoleau, that the Stanford library acquire the Foote letters. "It has long been my opinion that Mrs. Foote was one of the very best of the Western local color writers and her eminence as an illustrator gives her an additional distinction," he wrote.[7] At approximately the same time he was working on *Repose*, the University of California Press was preparing Foote's *Reminiscences* for publication.

Stegner wanted to use Foote's unpublished writing in *Repose* and approached Micoleau for permission. The now-famous correspondence has ambiguities on both sides. Stegner isn't entirely clear about his fictional intentions because he hasn't yet written the book. Micoleau, a civilian in the world of letters, finds herself corresponding with a famous novelist whose intentions seem vague.

STEGNER, writing about Foote and her husband, Arthur: "Of course it would not be a biography, and it would have to depart, when necessary—which might be often—from both facts of their careers and the facts of their characters."

MICOLEAU: "We'd be delighted to have the MHF materials used as background for a novel" and will make available "anything that you can use."[8]

After working for two years and having produced five hundred manuscript pages, Stegner resumed his correspondence with Micoleau.

STEGNER: "As I warned you, the process of making a novel from real people has led me to bend them where I had to, and you may not recognize your ancestors when I get through with them." He adds that "I have availed myself of your invitation to use the letters and 'Reminiscences' as I pleased, and so there are passages from both in my novel, *stolen outright*."[9]

7. Fradkin, *Wallace Stegner*, 231.
8. Fradkin, *Wallace Stegner*, 232.
9. Emphasis added.

He then offered to send her a copy of the draft manuscript.

MICOLEAU: "I'm glad you haven't abandoned the idea of the book . . . and I appreciate your thoughtfulness on consulting us again now that the ['Reminiscences'] are to be published. I see no need for you to change or modify anything." She politely declined Stegner's offer of a copy of his draft. "I'd just as soon wait until it is in print and easier to mail."[10]

In bending Mary H. Foote's story to his fictional devices, Stegner distorted her real life in significant ways. Some modern readers have detected a not-so-subtle suggestion by Stegner that Mary Foote had a sexual attraction to her best friend and epistolary soul mate, "Augusta Drake," as Stegner named her New York socialite friend Augusta DeKay. Stegner's character Susan Ward appears to have committed adultery with one of her husband's colleagues, an ardent admirer, and, while dallying with him on a picnic, leaves her infant daughter to drown. These plot elements were pure inventions.

After dipping into the published book, Micoleau again wrote to Stegner:

> You needn't fear that any of us will be offended—and I am sure I can speak for all of the family—by your blending of fiction with fact. I've read enough of it to know that this enhances the fascination of the book for me—discovering the threads of fact in the intricate pattern, while admiring the design and skill of the craftsman.[11]

Their exchange seems fairly straightforward, and their relationship might have ended there. Stegner comes off as honest and solicitous. Micoleau seems intelligent and obliging. Then all hell broke loose.

The opera was the proximate cause. Before opening night, *The San Francisco Chronicle* published what newspapers call a curtain-raiser—an article intended to generate interest in a forthcoming production. Blake Green's story, "The Genteel Western Lady Behind This Season's New Opera," introduced a new character into the *Repose* drama, another Foote granddaughter, Marian Foote Conway. She wasn't at all happy about the depiction of her ancestor in Stegner's novel.

10. Fradkin, *Wallace Stegner*, 241–42.
11. Fradkin, *Wallace Stegner*, 245.

Conway told the newspaper: "People who had barely known M. H. Foote would stop me on the street and say, in essence, 'I never knew your grandmother did *that!*'"

"That" referred to the adultery and involuntary infanticide. But, with the publication of Foote's writings, it became clear that Stegner had "borrowed" huge swatches of Foote's work, at times verbatim, from her letters and diaries. Stegner's two biographers estimate that either five percent of *Repose* (Jackson Benson) or ten per cent (Philip Fradkin) came straight from Foote. In 1982, Mary Ellen Williams Walsh, an English professor at Idaho State University, decided to publish an academic study of Stegner's sources in *Repose*. In a letter to Foote's granddaughter Conway, Walsh revealed her gut conclusion: "Stegner stole everything."[12]

According to Fradkin, Stegner complained of "the scurrilities of the Walsh woman" and considered suing.[13] In his recorded conversations with Richard Etulain, Stegner explained his irritation "at that particular holier-than-thou attack":

> [*Angle of Repose*] is a novel, not a biography. It has nothing to do with the life of Mary Hallock Foote except that I borrowed a lot of her experiences. So I don't, I guess, feel very guilty about that ... whenever fact will serve fiction—and I am writing fiction—I am perfectly willing to use it that way.[14]

He pointed out that he had once done the opposite, inserting the fictional story *Genesis* into his *Wolf Willow* memoir.

Had he been alive, Stegner might have been surprised to find the *Repose* controversy resurrected in 2022 by novelist/playwright Sands Hall, the daughter of Oakley Hall. In an essay for the California literary quarterly *Alta*,[15] Hall described how she researched the origins of *Repose* in 1998 to write a stage version of the novel that was never produced.

When she first heard that Stegner might have "borrowed" to write his famous novel, Hall "brushed away the idea that Stegner might be

12. Fradkin, *Wallace Stegner*, 259.

13. Fradkin, *Wallace Stegner*, 262.

14. Richard W. Etulain and Wallace Stegner, *Conversations with Wallace Stegner on Western History and Literature*, revised edition (Salt Lake City: University of Utah Press, 1990), 86–87.

15. Sands Hall, "The Ways of Fiction Are Devious Indeed," *Alta*, Apr. 4, 2022.

one of those men who'd arrogate a woman's work as his own." But on further investigation, she learned that "scene after scene drawn directly from [Mary Foote's] *Reminiscences* shows up in *Repose*, as do many lengthy verbatim quotes." Including, she noted, the title of Stegner's novel, lifted from a Mary Foote short story.

"Whose work of art is it, really?" Hall asked. She observed, sardonically, that when the novel appeared, "the *Atlantic* praised Stegner's ability with voice, especially Susan's, 'in letters that are a triumph of verisimilitude.'"

"*Verisimilitude.*
It's plagiarism."

Hall's essay gained extra visibility when novelist Roxana Robinson repurposed it for *The New Yorker*'s website a few months later.[16] Robinson didn't care for *Repose*; "Much of the prose seemed dull and airless, the scenes quotidian, and the dialogue wooden." After reading Foote's work, Robinson felt, "When I saw the plodding precision with which Stegner had rewritten scenes that Foote had already described, I understood the lifelessness of his writing." In her estimation, he was little more than a stenographer.

What do I think? I am perhaps more sympathetic to Stegner than I should be. *Repose* is not among my favorite books, or even my favorite Stegner novel. But the roots of fiction are hard to plumb. Many years ago, I found myself in the Massachusetts home of John Updike's editor, who told me Updike's neighbors lived in terror of finding themselves in his fiction: "He uses them all, all the time." It seems to me that Stegner dealt in good faith with Micoleau, whom he understood to be representing the Foote family's interests. Also, he championed Foote's work well before she became better known, after the 1972 publication of *Reminiscences.*

Autres temps, autres moeurs. Knowing Wally (at one remove) I suspect he would mount a spirited defense of his actions, were he alive to do so.

16. Roxana Robinson, "Wallace Stegner and the Trap of Using Other People's Writing," *New Yorker*, June 1, 2022, newyorker.com, accessed Sep. 15, 2024.

NINE

Crossing to Safety

"Never Get Old—it's a bummer."
—Wallace Stegner to Barry Lopez, 1986

Jackson Benson argues that Stegner's final four novels—*All the Little Live Things*, *Angle of Repose*, *The Spectator Bird*, and *Crossing to Safety*—constitute the author's "great period." *Repose*, we just saw, sits under a cloud. *Live Things* is a vivid social novel, transparently set in Los Altos Hills, with the retired, somewhat world-weary literary agent Joe Allston standing in for the increasingly Weltschmertz-stricken Stegner, as he also does in the intriguing *Spectator Bird*.

I'm not alone in thinking that Stegner's final novel, *Crossing to Safety*, might be his best. His daughter-in-law Lynn Stegner, herself a novelist, correctly observed (meaning that I agree with her) that "unlike many writers who blow their creative wad on an early novel (or novels) ... Stegner's work matured book by book, brick by brick, so that the fully gathered force and scope of his efforts over time amounted to a literary megalopolis."[1]

Allowing for some exaggeration on the part of a family member, it is true that Stegner's prose improved enormously over time, especially from the rough-hewn *Big Rock Candy Mountain* to the more smoothly turned *Crossing to Safety*. If he learned one thing in fiction, it was that stories didn't need "sweep" to be important. *Safety* is about two couples navigating the swells and shoals of academic life, with a dollop of inherited money thrown in. It is also about love, death, and

1. Wallace Stegner, "Introduction," in *On Teaching and Writing Fiction* (New York: Penguin, 2002), xi.

constancy—the latter probably being the strongest-held core value in Stegner's pantheon of personal behavior.

Here is a passage I love, describing an overflight of a flock of geese:

> Suddenly there they are, a wavering V headed directly over our hilltop, quite low, beating southward down the central flyway and talking as they pass. We stay quiet, suspending our human conversation until their garrulity fades and their quavering lines are invisible in the sky.
>
> They have passed over us like an eraser over a blackboard, wiping away whatever was there before they came.[2]

Sad to say, Stegner surrendered to some of his baser instincts in his final years. Fradkin noted more than once that Stegner could be quick to anger, and would cling, beaver-like, to a grudge, sometimes longer than a successful writer should. Younger writers supplant older writers, just as Stegner's beloved old forests have to yield to stronger rivals shooting up from the forest floor. Stegner's reputational decline—and his response to it—was not a becoming sight.

The lead-up to the 1976 publication of *The Spectator Bird* had some ominous portents for the 68-year-old Stegner. Like any publisher, Doubleday tried to smooth the path for its veteran author. Publicist Lucie Prinz wrote a letter to Harvey Shapiro, who had replaced John Leonard as the editor of the Sunday *Times Book Review*, pumping *Spectator Bird*: "I believe Stegner is our [Saul] Bellow, a major writer, a Pulitzer Prize winner, teacher, chronicler of his and his country's past," she wrote. "Stegner is less well known than he deserves. I hope that this book might change that."

Her plea landed in vain. Neither *The New York Times* nor the *Los Angeles Times* reviewed *The Spectator Bird.* Stegner wasn't bowled over by the reviews that did appear in *The Saturday Review* and *The New Yorker*, which he called "snippy." There is a note in Brandt & Brandt's files, urging its unidentified recipient to "Please pray!" for decent sales for Stegner's new book, which was not setting the world on fire. Brandt's British contact couldn't sell the book in the United Kingdom, and asked, "Am I right in thinking Wallace Stegner is a very old man? This novel reads as though he is, not just because of its

2. Wallace Stegner, *Crossing to Safety*, reprint edition (New York: Modern Library, 2002), 57.

subject matter but from its whole tone of rueful acceptance of age, and from the very leisurely pace."

The criticism might have been expected. For the second time, Stegner used the retired narrator Joe Allston to relate a story, this one buried in the past, in faraway Denmark, loosely based on a trip Wallace and Mary took in 1954. "I do think there is a generation gap," Stegner admitted to Carol Brandt. "In fact, I applaud it. Nobody under fifty is competent to review that magnificent book."[3]

It is better to be born lucky than to be born rich, and for the second time, lightning struck a struggling Stegner novel. *The Spectator Bird* won the National Book Award fiction prize for 1977, a surprise victor over rival works by former Stegner Fellow Raymond Carver and Ursula K. Le Guin. In its coverage, *The New York Times* was withholding, as usual, characterizing Stegner's win as "particularly controversial because none of the books nominated gained major public attention and several were not widely reviewed." The newspaper noted that "'The Spectator Bird' alternates between past and present and examines the difficult last years of life of a 69-year-old arthritic man."[4]

In a follow-up story, "Are the Judges Too Old?", *Times* critic Herbert Mitgang slathered more mud atop Stegner's victory. "The main criticism about the judges and their panels was that they had 'a little too much gray in their hair' and that therefore they favored older writers, and that they were not au courant with the latest fiction," he wrote. "It was Veteran's Day at Yankee Stadium," said one publisher, "The judges were out there rooting for Joe DiMaggio and Phil Rizzuto."[5]

The criticism didn't seem too far off the mark. One of the judges, the 74-year-old Erskine Caldwell, had commissioned Stegner's book *Mormon Country* thirty-five years earlier. Stegner also knew another judge, the former *New York Times* critic Orville Prescott, who, like Stegner, bemoaned "a huge generation gap between you and me and the writers and critics now in their forties and younger.

3. Philip Fradkin, *Wallace Stegner and the American West* (New York: Alfred A. Knopf, 2008), 275.

4. Herbert Mitgang, "Howe Gets History Book Award," *The New York Times*, Apr. 12, 1977.

5. Herbert Mitgang "Book Awards: Are the Judges Too Old?" *The New York Times*, Apr. 13, 1977.

They admire pretentious and unreadable experimentation in form, self-pitying exposures of emotional turmoil and intellectual confusion, and exploration of degeneracy."[6]

It is impossible to ignore the onset of spleen, or grouchiness, towards the end of Stegner's life. In essays and in public appearances, he lashed out at critics, real and imagined, occasionally besmirching his own good name. To what end, other than a dash of personal gratification, it is hard to say.

Take, for instance, the speech Stegner gave at the 1969 dedication of the J. Willard Marriott Library, where he would later donate his papers. Stegner's decision to site his archive at the University of Utah was already a political statement. Stanford, where he taught for twenty-five years and lived for almost a half century, was the more logical choice. Even though he had resigned in a huff, and, astonishingly, tried to remove his name from the famous Fellows program,[7] Northern California had become his spiritual home.

In a fit of pique prompted by Stanford's hiring of novelist Gilbert Sorrentino, whom Stegner called "a coterie writer of minimum distinction," he transferred his papers from the Stanford library, where they had been housed since 1976, and packed them off to Utah. "Stanford librarians, who simply assumed they would get the papers, were taken aback by his decision," according to Fradkin.[8] [9] "Any scholar who has to go to Salt Lake to study Stegner will get a bonus by being lured into good country," Stegner wrote to a friend.

Several years before the Sorrentino flap, Stegner used the dedication of the Marriott Library to unpack elements of his reactionary world view. "This is not the great age of books" he began—and took off from there. One initial beef: 1960s-era students had zero appreciation of history, ancient or modern. He invoked a conversation with a young student who inquired why Stegner had bothered to write *Wolf Willow*, a challenging minor masterpiece especially dear

6. Fradkin, *Wallace Stegner*, 277.

7. Fradkin, *Wallace Stegner*, 282 ff.

8. Fradkin, *Wallace Stegner*, 283.

9. Stegner hadn't always been a fan of his Utah alma mater. He was furious when the English department refused to promote him after he published the prize-winning *Remembering Laughter*. When his friend Phil Gray was eyeing a job there, Stegner described the U as "a cow college, but not a completely bad one."

to the writer's heart. "Why do you care where you came from or what your ancestors did? Isn't it what you ARE that matters? NOW?"

> Now. It is a big word with the young, almost as big a word as wow. Between them those two words seem sometimes to comprehend the responses of a whole generation.... The characteristic modern art form is the happening, which can't be programmed or repeated, but only joined in, participated in. Musicians celebrate silence over sound, or noise over music.

There is a discernible crankiness in the later novels, certainly in *Angle of Repose*, where the aging and infirm Lyman Ward has little use for his annoying son, a sociology professor whose sin is that he doesn't "get" history. "He irritates me," Lyman complains, "he always does. Nothing is interesting to him unless it's bellowing as loud as he is."[10] Ward, a self-described "Victorian," shares sexual mores with his literary creator: "I can't look upon marriage as anything but serious, or upon sex as casual or comic. I feel contempt for those who do so look upon it."[11]

Ward is taken aback by his young caregiver's penchant for not wearing a bra, which he describes more than once, in German ("ohne bustenhalter"), to preserve whose sensibilities it isn't clear at all. The effect in the novel is jarring and ridiculous, but probably not to Stegner.

Stegner told Etulain that the "hippie" character in *All the Little Live Things*, was just "a dumb bystander." "That was my feeling about hippies in general at that point," Stegner elaborated; "The ones that I knew then were dumb bystanders who didn't have any notion of what went on but thought they did."[12]

Hippies were far from the sole targets of Stegner's spleen. In his 1969 essay "Born a Square," Stegner unloaded on the tastemakers of the East. "Some part of our most advertised fiction," he writes, is

> sick, out of its mind, and out of the moral world, worshipful of Moloch, in love with decay and death. Another part is simply the corrupt answer to a corrupt demand, which is in turn cynically promoted. I do not

10. Wallace Stegner, *Angle of Repose* (New York: Vintage, 2014), 226.

11. Stegner, *Repose*, 564.

12. Richard W. Etulain and Wallace Stegner, *Conversations with Wallace Stegner on Western History and Literature*, revised edition (Salt Lake City: University of Utah Press, 1990), 75.

> mean "dirty" words or forthright scenes, sexual or otherwise; I speak of a necrophiliac playing with despair, which is nothing to be played with.

Stegner wonders out loud "if the characteristic American novelist of the 1960s won't turn out to be a Negro of the Jewish faith, born in Alabama and reared in Harlem and expatriated to Paris, where he picks up a living as a hustler in a homosexual joint"—which sounds like a paranoid and perverted miscegenation of James Baldwin and Norman Mailer.[13]

A self-pitying Stegner told Etulian that, after he left Harvard in 1945, "I more or less withdrew from American literature." That is nonsense—he published nine subsequent novels. He then moaned that "the more you stab your wife or throw big tantrums or big parties the more your literary reputation seems to grow"—a crude allusion to Mailer and Truman Capote, talented writers unworthy of his puerile kvetching.[14]

Under Stegner's pen, the vaunted "Western writer" sounds like Gary Cooper taking a bead on the depraved black hats of the New York literary axis. This hypothetical Western writer "had taken monogamy for granted, at least as a norm.... The fact is most Western writers don't feel at home in a literary generation that appears to specialize in despair, hostility, hypersexuality, and disgust."

Stegner even let some of this bile seep into his famous 1960 "Wilderness Letter." "Our literature ... is sick, embittered, losing its mind, losing its faith. Our novelists are the declared enemies of their society," he wrote.

> It seems to me significant that the distinct downturn in our literature from hope to bitterness took place almost at the precise time when the frontier officially came to an end, in 1890, and when the American way of life had begun to run strongly urban and industrial.

More nonsense, especially because his final novel, *Crossing to Safety*, is arguably his most intimate, his most hopeful, and his finest work.

The working title for *Crossing to Safety* was *Amicitia*, a nod to Cicero's *De Amicitia* (*On Friendship*), which explains the Romans'

---

13. Wallace Stegner, "Born a Square," in *The Sound of Mountain Water: The Changing American West* (New York: Vintage, 2017).

14. Etulain and Stegner, *Conversations*, 98, 99.

celebration of friendship as a kind of kinship, like the relationship between siblings. Looking back on his life, the Stegner-like narrator Larry Morgan says his most valued memories don't involve the books he'd written, or politics, but "details of friendship. . . . *Amicitia* lasts better than *res publica*, and at least as well as *ars poetica*."

Stegner borrowed the title from his friend Robert Frost's poem "I Could Give All to Time." In the verse, Frost discusses surrendering everything to Time, except what he has held on to "while the Customs slept." "Why declare," the poet asks, "the things I have crossed to Safety with?"

Safety is a thinly veiled account of the Stegners' long relationship with Phil and Peg Gray, the academic couple who introduced the Stegners to Greensboro, Vermont. As in the novel, the Grays (the Langs) were Greensboro grandees, longtime summer residents who sold the Stegners some land so their homes could be close together. "In a way that no book of mine ever has been, [*Crossing to Safety*] is an attempt to tell the absolute, unvarnished truth about other people and myself," Stegner said.[15] It succeeds.

Safety is an elegant, restrained novel. The "things" figuratively smuggled past Customs are friendship, memory, and love. "How do you make a book that anyone will read out of lives as quiet as these?" the Stegneresque narrator, Larry Morgan, asks. "Where are the things that novelists seize upon and readers expect? Where is the high life, the conspicuous waste, the violence, the kinky sex, the death wish?"

The 78-year-old Stegner naively hoped that the book would make him "rich and famous," he confided to a correspondent. Furthermore, "I am interested in seeing my reputation climb out of the hole the NY Times et-all [sic] dug for it."[16]

The *Times* loved the book, publishing not only a brief interview with Stegner, but also an elegiac review by author Doris Grumbach, who flat-out adored the novel. "What I am extolling here," she wrote

> is the appearance of a superb book at the other end of a consistently accomplished career, heartening proof that the novelist has continued to

15. Etulain and Stegner, *Conversations*, xi.
16. Fradkin, *Wallace Stegner*, 286.

> grow, is still maturing in his late maturity, has added to his accomplishments a sympathy for his contemporaries' condition: the miseries of old age, the resentment of physical decay and, most of all, the pleasures of enduring marital love.

This is the kind of "selling review" an author hopes will go on forever: "Mr. Stegner is a wise man as well as a skilled writer," Grumbach continued. "[He] has built a convincing narrative around this truth, has made survival a grace rather than a grim necessity, and enduring, tried love the test and proof of a good life."[17]

Safety, which principally takes place near the fictional Battell Pond in Vermont, feels like a very East Coast book, devoid of many of the themes Stegner had explored during his career, such as environmental depredation or stewardship of the land. "Without my intending it," he told a booksellers' group, "*Crossing to Safety* became, during the writing and rewriting of it, almost a *complaint* against the West ...

> against a liberty that too easily frays out into chaos, against the mobility that prevents a deep sense of family, community and place, against the brevity of time and the limited or attenuated nature of the group memory.[18]

The elderly Stegner was clearly warming to so-called traditional New England values. "There is something in Vermont—in its climate, people, history, laws—that wins people to it in love and loyalty," Stegner wrote in his 1981 book, *American Places*, "and does not welcome speculation and the unearned increment and the treatment of land and water as commodities. Here, if anywhere in the United States, land is a heritage as well as a resource, and ownership expresses stewardship, not exploitation."[19]

Vermont exercised another enchantment on Stegner. Unlike the arid West, which could become a dustbowl after only brief exposure to "civilization," Vermont could heal itself. You cut down the trees, they grow back. "This country *wants* to be trees"[20] he wrote, admiringly. After more than forty years of visiting the Green Mountain

17. Doris Grumbach, "The Grace of Old Lovers," *The New York Times*, Sep. 20, 1987.
18. Fradkin, *Wallace Stegner*, 285.
19. Wallace Stegner and Page Stegner, *American Places* (New York: Greenwich House, 1983), 55.
20. Stegner and Stegner, *Places*, 49.

State, "we have watched the north woods working quietly and inexorably to reclaim themselves, or part of themselves."[21]

Jackson Benson was surprised to learn that both Wallace and Mary planned to be buried in Greensboro. They share a headstone in Greensboro's Lincoln-Noyes cemetery; Wallace's ashes were scattered on a hillside near their cottage.

"This is a place you feel loyal about," Stegner told an interviewer shortly before his death. "Maybe it's because it's a stable community—the kind of community that I never lived in."[22]

When writing *Wolf Willow*, Stegner quoted his friend and student Wendell Berry's famous observation, "If you don't know where you are, you don't know who you are." Almost by default, Stegner had found his final home.

---

21. Stegner and Stegner, *Places*, 50.
22. Fradkin, *Wallace Stegner*, 322.

Afterword

"I really don't belong in the twentieth century."
—Wallace Stegner to Richard Etulain

What of Stegner now? On what would have been the author's 100th birthday, Timothy Egan re-hashed some of Stegner's beefs with the East Coast critics, yet concluded that "he's aged well—everywhere, perhaps, but Manhattan and Stanford, the cradle of the creative writing program he started."

Egan asked Tobias Wolff, author of *This Boy's Life* and a former Stegner fellow who teaches at Stanford, if the university offered a class on Stegner. Perhaps predictably, the answer was no. "Generally, students don't read him here," Wolff told Egan. "I wish they would."[1]

Roughly ten years later, *New York Times* critic A. O. Scott re-appreciated Stegner in a lengthy essay, "Wallace Stegner and the Conflicted Soul of the West." Scott, a fan, waxed realistic about Stegner's afterlife. Re-affirming Wolff's earlier assessment, he noted that Stegner's name didn't appear on college syllabuses or in the Library of America. "Stegner's books," he wrote, "abide in an under-visited stretch of the American canon, like a national park you might drive past on the way to a theme park or ski resort."[2]

Stegner believed himself to be a chronicler of eternal verities, but verities are always under assault.

Elizabeth Cook-Lynn, a member of the Crow Creek Sioux Tribe and a professor emerita at Eastern Washington University, made a small splash with her 1996 book, *Why I Can't Read Wallace Stegner and Other Essays: A Tribal Voice.* She objected, for instance, to

1. Timothy Egan, "Stegner's Complaint," *The New York Times*, Feb. 18, 2009.
2. A. O. Scott, "Wallace Stegner and the Conflicted Soul of the West," *The New York Times*, June 1, 2020.

Stegner's phrase "If I am native to anything, I am native to this," when he described the Cypress Hills country of Saskatchewan in *Wolf Willow*. "Stegner simply claims indigenousness," she wrote,[3] although he is clearly writing about his personal story and his lifelong search for a place to call home. Cook-Lynn also attacked Stegner's statement to Etulian that "Western history sort of stopped in 1890," and that "the Plains Indians were done." She pointed out that the Plains Indians are living their history up to the present day, with considerable difficulties placed in their way by white men.

Wolf Willow, in fact, devoted some attention to the Plains Indians, who found shelter from the American cavalry north of the U.S.–Canada border, which the Stegners' farm abutted on its south side. Stegner also examined the history of the indigenous Canadian Indians within the history of southern Saskatchewan. That said, it is hardly surprising that a book written in 1962 doesn't satisfy the expectations of a purportedly more enlightened generation. Whatever the case, Stegner isn't here to defend his work.

The "under-appreciated Stegner" chorus is always in full throat. A significant coterie of literary critics have always viewed John Steinbeck, another unreconstructed Westerner, as undervalued, but stories that look simple on their surface often prove to be complex. With his vocal support of the Vietnam War, Steinbeck courted the disdain of the liberal East Coast panjandrums, yet he was certainly one of the country's best-known novelists when he won the Nobel Prize for Literature in 1957. And who says American readers don't appreciate Western writers with a literary bent? Ken Kesey planted his flag west of the Rockies, and Larry McMurtry flourished west of Stegner's cherished 100th meridian. While McMurtry's reputation was burnished by marvelous Hollywood adaptations of his work—*Hud*, *The Last Picture Show*, and *Terms of Endearment* (to say nothing of the TV series *Lonesome Dove*)—it's certainly arguable that McMurtry was equally prolific, and a better writer than Stegner, or at least a more modern storyteller.

When Egan published his 100th-birthday article, novelist Jane Smiley, herself a Western writer, commented that "every writer in

3. Elizabeth Cook-Lynn, *Why I Can't Read Wallace Stegner and Other Essays: A Tribal Voice* (Madison, WI: University of Wisconsin Press, 1996), 29–30.

America could make the case that he or she is a bit ignored or underrated or misapprehended."

> The land is big, and every vista looks different from every other. There is no spot in the US that epitomizes what it is to be American, and that is a wonderful thing about American literature.... The flip side of this "obscurity" is, for the reader, a repeated sense of discovery, not just of authors, but of places. That is our pleasure.

It's possible that Stegner lost points with posterity for refusing to cleave to one genre. He was a bracingly talented non-fiction writer and biographer, but saw himself as a novelist first and a historian and advocate second. The progressive unspooling of his literary ability is also unusual, and hard to parse. Readers bridle, with cause, at the leaden prose of *The Big Rock Candy Mountain* and the occasional drudgery of plowing through *Angle of Repose*. But Stegner proved himself as a lyrical writer of supernal sensitivity in his final novel. It took him a lifetime to get there.

In his conversations with Etulain, Stegner described himself as an "old-fashioned novelist." Stegner provided an elaboration that could have sprung from Henry Adams's pen:

> I said I felt like a nineteenth-century anachronism, and I still feel a little that way. I really don't belong in the twentieth century; I grew up in the nineteenth century, even though it was technically on the calendar as the twentieth.... What I was growing up in was 1914 Saskatchewan, but in its development, it was about like 1860 Kansas.... I never saw a water closet or a bathtub till I was twelve years old. I never saw a lawn until I was twelve years old.[4]

What has Wallace Stegner attempted to leave for his readers? Etulain asked. "Oh boy!" Stegner replied. "You're now looking for a philosophical residue, the sludge in the bottom of the cup." He speculated that his writing career was in some sense "a sort of hangover from Presbyterian Sunday School. When I was young, I got little badges and then little wreaths around wreaths for never having missed Sunday School for seven years."

---

4. Richard W. Etulain and Wallace Stegner, *Conversations with Wallace Stegner on Western History and Literature*, revised edition (Salt Lake City: University of Utah Press, 1990), 197.

I suppose that must have marked me in some curious and unpleasant way. . . . I suppose that I'm constantly trying to bear in mind that having been very lucky, I also am very responsible, and that the only thing that makes civilization go forward is the responsibility of individuals, whether gifted or otherwise, small or large. All of us have the obligation somehow to have some kind of concern for the species, for the culture, for the larger thing outside of ourselves. I'm sure that's buried not too deeply in most of the books I've written.[5]

5. Etulain and Stegner, 196.

Acknowledgments

I am very grateful to Gary Bergera, the former editor of this series, for welcoming my suggestion of a non-Mormon subject, Wallace Stegner. Members of the LDS Church effectively raised Stegner in Salt Lake City, where he attended high school and the University of Utah. Stegner admired the core values of Mormon culture and would be delighted to be included in a group of books about LDS notables.

Stegner's papers reside at the J. Willard Mariott Library at the University of Utah and the Special Collections staff helped me enormously during a 2022 visit. Special thanks to manuscripts archivist Kristina Lynae Barksdale and Gina Giang for their valuable help. Many thanks to my friends Mark Feeney and Kirsten Lundberg for reading successive drafts of this manuscript, improving it significantly.

As a longtime reader of Signature Books, I am delighted to become one of their authors. Thank you to John Hatch, Jason Francis, and Martha Bradley-Evans at the Smith–Pettit Foundation, for making this project happen.

Index

About the Author

Alex Beam has written two novels and seven works of non-fiction, two of them *New York Times* Notable Books of the Year. In 2014, he published *American Crucifixion*, a narrative history of the assassination of the Mormon prophet Joseph Smith. *The Wall Street Journal* called it "an excellent book about the life and death of an utterly uncategorizable man."

A longtime columnist for *The Boston Globe*, Beam lives with his family in Newton, Massachusetts.